Consecrated Religious Life

THE CHANGING PARADIGMS

Consecrated Religious Life

THE CHANGING PARADIGMS

DIARMUID O'MURCHU, MSC

ORBIS  BOOKS
Maryknoll, New York 10545

Founded in 1970, Orbis Books endeavors to publish works that enlighten the mind, nourish the spirit, and challenge the conscience. The publishing arm of the Maryknoll Fathers and Brothers, Orbis seeks to explore the global dimensions of the Christian faith and mission, to invite dialogue with diverse cultures and religious traditions, and to serve the cause of reconciliation and peace. The books published reflect the views of their authors and do not represent the official position of the Maryknoll Society. To learn more about Maryknoll and Orbis Books, please visit our website at www.maryknoll.org.

Library of Congress Cataloging-in-Publication Data

Ó Murchú, Diarmuid.
    Consecrated religious life: the changing paradigms / Diarmuid O'Murchu.
        p. cm.
    Includes bibliographical references.
    ISBN 1-57075-619-8 (pbk.)
        1. Monasticism and religious orders—Rules. 2. Monastic and religious life.
3. Catholic Church—Clergy. I. Title.
BX2436.O48 2005
255--dc22

                                                     2005003886

CONTENTS

PREFACE

In 1960, there were over 1,300,000 Religious in the Catholic Church. Forty years later in 2000, the number had declined to 900,000.

Throughout the 1970s and 1980s, observers suggested that this was a Western, white phenomenon, one that was unlikely to impact on the two-thirds world. Some even boldly predicted that increasing vocations in the South would outpace the decline in the West, and that missionaries from the South would end up evangelizing Europe.

As we entered the 1990s, the first indications of decline were noted in both Asia and South America. In both continents the declining pattern is now much more apparent, with indications that a similar trend is beginning to unfold in various countries of the African subcontinent.

How Do We Name the Crisis?

When I and others first predicted this trend in the 1970s, we were quickly dismissed as prophets of doom. In fact, we were only trying to honor the history of Religious Life with its consistently unfolding cycle of rise and decline. For the majority of historians this spells a kind of historical fatalism, but for those who view history in a more spiritual context, the evidence is that of an evolutionary process of birth-death-rebirth, which calls for creative imagination and profound discernment.

The current model of Religious Life seems to have served its purpose and, therefore, large-scale decline—a metaphorical Calvary experience—is both necessary and desirable as a prerequisite for a new Resurrection moment. As in previous historical cycles, this may involve the revitalization, or refounding, of some traditional Orders and Congregations, but it will also involve the extinction of many groups which exist today.

One thing is certain: *Religious Life will continue to flourish*—but not without a huge divesting of the accretions of time and culture. The wealth we have accumulated, the status and privilege we have amassed, the fame we have accrued, will have to be shed. But most disturbing of all, our strong allegiance to institutional Catholicism is among the false securities we will also have to dispense with.

We will be stripped of all the baggage we have accumulated—culturally and ecclesiastically—and when once more we are disposed to travel light, the Spirit will blow through the dead bones (Ez 37:1-14) and new life will evolve where we least expect it. The paradox of Calvary and Resurrection will be our hardest cross to bear but also our greatest hope for the future.

A Time to be Born – A Time to Die!

The current model of Religious Life has another 60-80 years before it will be sufficiently emptied out for the creative Spirit to breathe afresh. What this book depicts are some of the transitions we will be asked to endure in that intervening time. We will have to let go of time-honored traditions that hinder the call to prophetic witness (Chapter Two). We will need great wisdom and courage to discern which apostolic options are likely to serve us best if we are to remain loyal to the vision of the Kingdom of God (Chapter Three). And, finally, our enduring hope rests in the new future the Spirit evokes in each new era (Chapter Four).

In the Third Chapter of the book, I offer some tentative suggestions on what the new vision might look like. Its true *gestalt* (shape), however, belongs to the creativity of the divine Spirit, and not to human projections—from me or anybody else—no matter how spiritually inspired they may be.

Our Future Hope

The material of this book falls between faithful realism and enduring hope. We need to face our diminution with honesty and integrity, if for no other reason than it will enable us to die with dignity, and that has important witness-value in a world where undignified death is so widespread. True Christian hope does not evade the inevitability of death, but knows it as a necessary stage for Resurrection promise and new life.

On the basis of that promise we can glean something of what the future will look like. Whether my Congregation, or any other, is to live or die, is not for us humans to decide. That is in the hands of the creative Spirit who guarantees the future of Religious Life and has consistently birthed new groups to sustain that future. More than anything else this is a time for radical trust in the paradoxical nature of divine creativity.

Religious Life has changed dramatically in the past 40 years. The Christian churches, especially, the Catholic Church, seek in vain to stabilize the changing trends and establish definitive models. I suspect that for us, Religious, the biggest changes are ahead of us, not behind us. And I hope that this book, in however small a way, will prepare us to deal in a more creative and discerning way with the dramatic changes that will characterize the vowed life for the rest of the 21st century.

While I was asked to write this book to encourage men and women Religious in the Philippines, I hope it can do the same for Religious everywhere. Filipino Religious are now experiencing the decline more of us have known since the 1960s; in some Congregations, vocations have fallen sharply. My hope is that the reflections of this book will give context to what is happening there and elsewhere: openness rather than denial in the face of decline, serenity rather than confusion as the transition unfolds, and above all, vision and hope to embrace a new and different future.

WHAT HAVE PARADIGMS GOT TO DO WITH RELIGIOUS LIFE?

Consecrated persons therefore must keep themselves as intellectually open and as adaptable as possible, so that the apostolate will be envisaged and carried out according to the needs of their own time, making use of the means provided by cultural progress.

VITA CONSECRATA (VC 71)

As a cultural concept a *paradigm* refers to a dominant model out of which we act and behave on a daily basis. These are some of the paradigms that prevail in the contemporary world:

- God rules from on high.
- Governance is mediated through hierarchical systems—we govern from the top down.
- Information is transmitted from the teacher to the pupil.
- Genes govern and control behavior.
- Progress happens through the survival of the fittest.

- Religion/the Church is responsible for morality.
- Christianity is based on divine revelation and its truths are beyond question.
- The wisdom of science is more reliable than that of religion.
- We earn money by working for it.

Scholars will argue at great length about this selective list. Some will try to claim that the issue of governance based on hierarchy and the religious statements I make are blueprints given to us by God and, therefore, will never change, nor should they ever be tampered with. Countering this argument, postmodernists will claim that so-called revealed truths are true within the perceptions and understandings of a particular group of people at a specific time in history and, therefore, can never claim a once-for-all veracity.

Changing Models

To launch our reflections on paradigm shifts I want to reflect on the issue of a working wage and the accompanying notion of a work ethic. Earning money through work or labor is something we take for granted and rarely reflect on why we do it this way. It illustrates three different paradigms over a timespan of about 300 years. As recently as the 1800s, people were still living out of a barter-economy in which goods were exchanged for other goods rather than for money. Animals were exchanged for raw-products; or the produce of the land was exchanged for clothing. Using money as remuneration for work was relatively unknown.

For much of the 20th century, doing work to earn money became the norm, despite the fact that in several countries more than 50% of the population worked in the "informal economy" (housewives, students, elderly people; voluntary workers, artists, musicians) and did not earn a standard wage. Making work synonymous with money is a relatively recent phenomenon, with a far more direct application in the white Western world than elsewhere. That work is an expression of human creativity, and a necessary outlet for human growth and happiness, is a notion long known to our species. Now that work and money have become so synonymous we face a growing human dilemma of alienation and unhappiness. Firstly, the work people do in order to earn money is frequently tedious, boring and tiring; rather than enhance creativity it often undermines it. Secondly, with paid work as the norm for being "successful," millions in our world feel disempowered.

As in other spheres of modern life, work, too, assumes a different meaning. We are now moving into a new paradigm popularly known as contract labor, part-time work in which people are paid by the hour, with little back-up security such as pension schemes or health insurance. The job-for-life is a fast-fading ideal, once more throwing many people into confusion, activating new levels of insecurity and uncertainty.

Here we can distinguish, not just three modifications to a prevailing work ethic, but three very different understandings of what work means. The model of the 1800s is largely that of a *gift-economy*, wherein an unarticulated sense of the giftedness of everything dictates a system of exchange between people. The second, typical of Western nations in the 20th century, is closer to a *reward-economy*, but very much to the advantage of those who score best in a Capitalistic system. The third shift includes a conscious disillusionment with the previous model and a largely unarticulated desire to separate money from work once more so that everybody can exercise their creative potential through meaningful work—whether paid or not. Idealistic though it may sound, what we are aspiring to here may be described as a *creativity-economy*. In fact, it is the economic ordering that humans have known for most of their time on this earth.

What is of interest and significance in these examples, as with all paradigm shifts, is that no one person, organization or government decided to change from one model to another. We are dealing with an organic evolutionary development, which often defies human logic, and tends to be ridiculed by those who subscribe to the belief that humans are in charge of creation and, therefore, all developments in human culture are, to one degree or another, brought about by human agency.

Is there a theoretical basis for these views? The seminal work of Thomas Kuhn is the one most frequently cited, and of course, Kuhn is not without his critics. Much of Kuhn's work is about the shift from one scientific worldview to another. An obvious example from science is the shift from the classical, mechanistic model of the 17th century to the quantum relational model which began to unfold in the 1920s and is still the basis of research and controversy.

A useful contemporary example is that of healthcare. Mainstream medicine tends to adopt the mechanistic model as a foundational way of working. When a doctor examines a patient s(he) is trying to assess what has gone wrong with a particular part of the anatomy and what interventions need to be made to correct it. The underlying principle here asserts that the whole equals the sum of the parts and, therefore, the challenge is to rectify the faulty or damaged part.

A doctor using the complementary (alternative), holistic approach adopts a radically different approach based on the principle that the whole is greater than the sum of the parts. The presenting symptoms or illness is a pointer to some kind of imbalance in the overall health of the organism. Therefore the overall state of well-being, or lack of it, becomes the primary target of investigation. Lifestyle, diet, stress, relationships, toxic influences from the environment, spiritual outlook, are all investigated in the hope of discerning deleterious ways of behaving leading to the symptoms or illness. Return to health will require some radical changes at the larger level and not just the eradication of the observable symptoms. This is broadly known as the holistic approach, one that gains increasing credibility in the modern Western world. Of course, it has been practiced by indigenous healers for several millennia, long before modern medicine became so mechanized.

Checking our Assumptions

What we are really dealing with is the issue of cultural assumptions. As a human species we are always operating with inherited assumptions and we are always changing them in the light of new cultural insights. Some assumptions come to the fore and can prevail as dominant guidelines for a number of decades, centuries or even millennia. They become standard beliefs or cultural paradigms. The longer they have prevailed the more unassailable they will be in terms of challenge or change. Briefly, I wish to review two assumptions rarely named or acknowledged for their influence and impact: the first is *patriarchy* and the second, *anthropocentrism.*

1. *Patriarchy.* Possibly the most enduring of all assumptions is the conviction that the human mind is unassailable and, therefore, life on our planet can be subjected to human reason, scrutiny and control. This conviction favors the strong, the wealthy and the powerful. This way of thinking is in fact relatively recent, very much the product of patriarchal times dating back   •
about 8,000 years.

To our contemporary minds, 8,000 years is almost incomprehensible and that perception embodies one of the most destructible and crippling assumptions we humans work with. What we find at work here is the all-powerful hand of patriarchy for which *control* is a central value. What happened over the past 2,000 years we can control reasonably well. Therefore, we often regard the 2,000 year benchmark to be the beginning of everything of importance in our lives; this is particularly true for Christians.

Academics, on the other hand, stretch the patriarchal measuring rod a bit further. They find classical Greek culture immensely attractive, particularly its emphasis on rationality, logic and the priority of the male over the female. But their ultimate horizon is the rise of *civilization*, characterized by the development of writing in ancient Sumerian culture and the rise of the first cities, both of which are dated to 3,500 BCE. Cultural developments before that time are deemed to be uncivilized, primitive and barbaric to one degree or another.

What I am trying to highlight is the reductionism and destructiveness of the central tenets of the patriarchal world view which chooses to ignore our evolutionary timespan of 6,000,000 years and focuses all the attention on the narrow, functional developments of the most recent 5 to 10 millennia. All of us have been indoctrinated to regard the patriarchal paradigm as normal and normative, as insuperable and eternal. But it is precisely that paradigm that is beginning to crumble and disintegrate, and that more than anything else is what generates so much interest in the subject of paradigms today.

What we have inherited from the reign of patriarchy is a culture of fierce competition in which the strategy of divide-and-conquer has run amok. It has left us with a rather violent world, a carved-up planet and an exploited environment. The yearning for a different way of being, the consciousness that begets the possibility of a different paradigm began to surface strongly after the Second World War. We note its emergence in the creation of the United Nations in the 1940s. Subtle, subconscious forces were at work, drawing nations into new alliances, fomenting greater cooperation and interdependence. Since then, it has also become a great deal more apparent that the major issues facing humanity today, especially regarding ecological and environmental threat, and more recently, global security, can only be addressed and managed by international bodies and not by individual states. The nation state is becoming weaker and weaker, a demise we bemoan and presume to be potentially dangerous and undesirable.

2. *Anthropocentrism.* What prevents us from embracing the big picture of reality and thus honoring creation in a much more open and engaging way? The short answer is anthropocentrism, a second major assumption requiring urgent attention. Anthropocentrism is one of the most resilient and stubborn belief systems ever adopted by the human species and is the major barrier to seeing paradigm shifts for what they really are. It basically states that things are as we humans understand them to be, and things can only develop as we dictate. The molding of reality is in our hands. The Copenhagen interpretation of the Quantum theory adopts this line of argument. Some social scientists claim that

anthropocentrism is insuperable because it is so deeply rooted in the patriarchal worldview.

Consequently, only those changes augmented and directed by humans can be objectively verified and these alone are worthy of serious investigation. Talk about paradigm shifts is too big, amorphous and beyond human control. Therefore, it is of no interest to humans and is widely assumed to be of no consequence for our future progress.

It is not within the scope of this book to offer a refutation of the anthropocentric worldview, nor is a social scientist like myself, especially one influenced by spiritual values, likely to be taken seriously in offering such a counter view. I will proceed, therefore, by outlining the main features on which the notion of paradigm shifts begins to make sense:

1. Nothing in creation is static. Evolution keeps everything moving in a dynamic way.

2. Growth requires change; without change things begin to stagnate and will never reach their full potential.

3. The notion that progress happens in a gradual linear fashion mainly through the mechanism of the survival of the fittest, is a Darwinian viewpoint, widely endorsed by the scientific community but disputed in several other fields of contemporary wisdom.

4. Several things influence the patterns of change in creation at large and most of these are beyond human control.

5. Religionists suggest that the activation of change is totally in God's hands, leaving humans in a somewhat passive role.

6. Both science and religion espouse the central values of patriarchy, and, consequently, comprehend in a shortsighted and distorted way what activates and guides the forces of change in the world.

7. Change is neither random nor deterministic. In many aspects of nature it is cyclic, and to the naïve viewer would seem to be going nowhere, lacking all sense of direction. It is also paradoxical, often with apparent contradictions and a great deal of suffering and pain. But perhaps, more notable than anything else is the growth in complexity as creation unfolds over the long aeons. This is the vital clue that leads to a sense of meaning.

8. Social scientists are reluctant to talk of progress in evolution, but they are prepared to talk about a preferred sense of direction, and here they are alluding to the growth in complexity. With this comes a sense of advancement and greater transparency to an underlying sense of mystery which seems to be ultimately benign and not destructive.

9. Several of these ideas come together in the notion of the paradigm shift. It describes a major change or shift in direction, not obviously instigated by humans, and often bewildering and confusing for humans. An old understanding begins to fall apart and lose credibility even while still extensively used

by humans. Forces seem to be at work that defy human logic and can begin to feel like a major threat to human management and control.

10. Initially, the shift meets with much resistance. It may be ridiculed or demonized. In time, even some of its strongest opponents come on board although rarely will they acknowledge that they have changed their views, principles or values.

11. Are humans therefore, at the mercy of these shifting patterns? It seems like we have two choices in the face of paradigm shifts: resist—in which case we are likely to become the helpless victims of something that will feel progressively more alienating. The alternative is that we learn to flow with the change and in that case we stand a much better chance of becoming its creative beneficiaries.

12. The crucial issues, therefore, are those of human perception and the consequent understanding of:

   a)   How creation works in evolutionary terms.

   b)   How we see ourselves within the global evolutionary process.

   c)   How we understand the process of creation, and our role within it, from a spiritual perspective.

   d)   Where we stand with the ideology of anthropocentrism.

The concept of the paradigm shift defies a great deal of human rationality and certainly transcends many of the conventional ways in which we view reality today. Perhaps, more than anything else we need a holistic spirituality to comprehend with the depth and breadth that this concept requires of us. All of which should indicate that those in the vowed life should be more amenable to this deeper understanding. But we, too, have been conditioned by time and culture, and the invitation to this new way of seeing requires for many of us a big conversion of heart and mind.

Jesus and a New Paradigm

The Christian gospels are replete with paradigm shifts. While many scholars highlight the Jewishness of Jesus and his allegiance to his inherited faith and culture, it is difficult to avoid the earthshaking revolution he proclaimed and lived. A vivid example, not immediately obvious to readers of the Gospels, is the Beatitudes in which those declared blessed are the very ones marginalized and disempowered by the prevailing culture and social norms. And in the Sermon on the Mount (Matthew, Chapters 5-7), we find some intriguing examples of changing paradigms:

a) *Turn the other cheek.* "If anyone strikes you on the right cheek, turn the other also" (Mt 5:39). This means the person striking now must use the left cheek and this will require using the left hand which in Jewish culture was considered a ritually unclean act which no self-respecting Jew would want to perform. In other words, you have disempowered the one trying to exert violent power over you. The alternative would be to use the backhand, which in the culture of Jesus was commonly used to force somebody into subjection because the person posed a threat by retaining their sense of equality. Jesus is advocating acts of defiance, offering alternative behavioral models, rendering a powerful one incapable of asserting dominance over another. A new paradigm of liberation and empowerment is being invoked.

b) *Go the extra mile.* "And if anyone forces you to go one mile, go with him two miles" (Mt 5:41). The ancient Persians required their soldiers to carry their packs until they dropped of exhaustion. The Romans, trying to procure a more benign image, limited this test of endurance to one mile, and had their roads marked clearly for this purpose. Here Jesus encourages his followers to call the bluff of this outer respectability by going the extra mile and consequently getting the Roman commander into trouble for not abiding by the rules. The tables are turned, as a new paradigm requires new relationships in which we are all challenged to treat each other with dignity and transparency.

c) *Give away your cloak.* "And if anyone would sue you and take your coat, let him have your cloak as well" (Mt 5:40). The context here is a courtroom in which a creditor could take as collateral a person's outer robe, but it had to be returned each evening so that the poor man would have something in which to sleep. Jesus is advocating that the person also give the inner garment, thus leaving oneself completely naked. Nakedness was taboo in Judaism and the ensuing shame fell on the one that caused the nakedness rather than on its victim. By stripping the debtor, shame has been brought upon the creditor. He has been shamed into seeing the cruelty of his demands. It is not the poor man who has been humiliated but the creditor. Jesus advocates subversiveness to reclaim dignity and self-worth.

These examples illuminate the paradigm shift that Jesus initiated in his day. Jesus proclaims a new way of relating, an alternative to power and dominance. This is nowhere so graphically illustrated as in the parables and miracles. Here Jesus confronts the conventional norms, especially those of inclusion and exclusion—who is considered worthy to be in and who must be kept out—and consistently breaks down all the barriers associated with impurity, unworthiness and exclusion. Prostitutes and sinners are included at the table; the rabble are welcome to the wedding feast; the tax-collector stands inside the temple door, not outside it; all the workers are rewarded for laboring in the vineyard; and it takes a radically excluded one, namely a Samaritan, to render to an "impure" person one of the greatest acts of inclusion recorded in the Gospels.

Jesus turned upside-down the culture of his day. He

released a new paradigm that was as shocking as it was original. The early Church quickly domesticated and tamed that prophetic vision. Christendom over some 2,000 years has worked hard to habituate it and even accommodate it to several patriarchal regimes. In our day, that prophetic vein is coming into its own once more, and as I shall indicate throughout this book, I believe it is one of the primary functions of the vowed life to honor and reclaim that Gospel subversiveness. In the words of Joan Chittister (1995, 2): "The fact is that Religious Life was never meant simply to be a labor force in the church; it was meant to be a searing presence, a paradigm of search, a mark of human soul and a catalyst to conscience in the society in which it emerged."

Application to Religious Life[1]

The conventional paradigm of the vowed life exhibits a number of widely recognized features which include:

1. The world is a sinful and dangerous place from which we need to flee if we want to be sure of our eternal salvation.

2. Spirituality is essentially a battle in a dualistic world in which good is forever trying to overcome evil.

3. Most people are involved in the affairs of the world. Some, however, have received a vocational calling—firstly, priests, secondarily, Religious—making salvation accessible for themselves and serving as a model for how others can reach salvation.

4. Salvation requires us to mortify and subdue the body with its dangerous instincts and desires. Incessant prayer, penance and asceticism are the chief means through which we do this.

5. The world needs powerful reminders (vowed people) of the transitory nature of earthly life. Religious serve as an eschatological sign of the life to come which is where all our hopes will be fulfilled.

6. Therefore the internal structuring of the vowed life must emulate as closely as possible the way we believe things are in the heavenly realm: highly ordered, prayerful, asexual, and harmonious according to the wishes of the ruling God.

7. The spirituality of the vowed life is essentially an ascetical one of suffering and sacrifice: "It is in the contemplation of the crucified Christ that all vocations find their inspiration" (VC 23).

8. Fulfillment of one's vocation is judged by the observance of the Rule and the Constitutions in lifelong fidelity to God and to the Church.

What I allude to as the old paradigm, despite its strong emphasis on prayer and devotion, was strongly based on the observance of externalized rules, laws and expectations. This is essentially a masculine model in which performance is all important. You are judged by others—and end up judging yourself—by what you achieve in a quantifiable and measurable way. Even spiritual growth tends to be judged in terms of the frequency of spiritual "exercises."

Most people alive in Religious Life today were formed in this model, and, tragically, it is still widely adopted, albeit in an updated form in the formation of younger Religious in Africa and Asia. Moreover, documents from Rome (e.g. *Vita Consecrata*) still adopt this ascetical, patriarchal approach; even the language used betrays an allegiance to it. Many people object to what they deem to be a harsh and unnecessary criticism in the way I am naming the old paradigm. To the extent that they agree about it being an old model, they would prefer we let it die peacefully rather than "attack" it. After all, they say, this is the model that produced saintly and heroic people who rendered unsurpassable service to God and to humanity. For that very reason, some feel we should be trying to rescue it, rather than undermining it.

This is where the analysis arising from the discernment around paradigm shifts is qualitatively different from other ways of understanding. The paradigmatic approach is far more organic and seeks to honor the paradoxical process of evolution as everything goes through the cycle of birth-death-rebirth. Indeed, the history of Catholic Religious Life verifies this in a clear and convincing way, but most Church historians, educated in a rational factual pedagogy, tend not to see the richness and depth of the cyclic approach.[2] This alternative discernment seeks to be more transparent in naming the cultural and timebound contexts in which things arise, along with the symptoms of cultural decline signalling that particular cultural expressions have outlived their usefulness. In a world so scared of death and letting-go, advocates of new paradigms see death as something natural and healthy for everything—including religions and their major institutions—so that the option of rebirth can be realized.

Implicit in these observations is the acknowledgement that what I call the "old paradigm" was once a valid vibrant model, and indeed may still be useful but with a reduced cultural relevance. To try and keep it valid for all time effectively turns what was meant to be fluid and organic into something rigid and ideological. It becomes a god unto itself, cumbersome, calcified, draining creative energy for its maintenance—energy that should be put at the service of new life and mission.

A Time for Letting Go!

Ours is a time of paradigms-in-transition, with many among us locked in denial in the face of the demise of the old models. At so many levels of contemporary life previous ways of relating to reality and former functional models are proving to be irrelevant, and in many cases, useless. Clinging to the past, we hold on to old baggage, and this enslaves us, diminishing our freedom to embrace the new future. In this in-between time, the call to authentic discernment carries a heavier responsibility than at any other time. These are some of the reasons:

1. As human beings we tend to feel more secure with the familiar and with what we know intimately.

Our natural desire, therefore, is to cling to the old. Since cultural institutions tend to be self-perpetuating, when confronted with the challenge to change, they tend to become so rigidly resistant that they frequently capitulate their own perdition. Individual members within a collectivity (in this case, a Religious Order) or subgroups within a larger body (various Orders within a denominational Church), will find it extremely difficult to honor their desire to change within the restraining pull of the larger body.

2. Because of the patriarchal nature of all our major institutions, in the face of change we tend to look to the institution and its higher authority for guidance and wisdom. Naively, we expect change to come from the top down. But it rarely does. Instead it tends to come from the bottom up. The rank-and-file will change long ahead of the institutions and their leaderships.

3. Paradigmatic change is even more complex. It is instigated neither by people at the top nor at the base. Evolutionary dynamics are at work here, beyond the control of human beings and even at times beyond human comprehension. Darwinians will explain this as a random process in which nature will select what is right for the emergent moment, deleting what is not useful in the process. This is a rather mechanistic interpretation congruent with the classical science of the past 400 years. But it has the value of alerting us to a radical freedom within cre-

ation, not random however, nor governed solely by natural selection. Theologically, we are encountering the free and daring Spirit of God who blows where she wills, bringing order out of chaos as at the dawn of creation.

4. Here we encounter the great paradox of all change whether personal, systemic or global: there can be no Resurrection (radical fresh possibility) without a catalyzing Calvary (a radical letting-go, a painful death experience). And this is the supreme piece of discernment for which Christians generally seem to be poorly equipped. Firstly, it requires as Brueggemann (1978; 1986) reminds us, the facility to engage with the numbness of death, the ability to grieve and lament, and thus be freed from our attachments to what feels safe and familiar. How do we do our collective and institutional grieving? And perhaps most importantly of all, how do we embrace the painful, but liberating task of burying the dead?

Today, in the West, several Religious Orders and Congregations are dying out. Yet, nobody, it seems, wants to talk about death. We continue to plunge ourselves into reactive depression, rather than embrace proactive letting-go. And nobody seems to have any sense of what "burying the dead" might actually mean in our circumstances. It looks like there will be a lot of repressed grief around for some years ahead, which is the very thing that may prevent us from being refounded in our Orders and Congregations.

Embracing a Different Future

In the document, *Vita Consecrata*, we read: "Institutes of consecrated life are thus invited courageously to propose anew the enterprising initiative, creativity and holiness of their founders and foundresses in response to the signs of the times emerging in today's world" (VC 37). Almost twenty years earlier, the document, *Mutuae Relationes* (No. 19), affirms that ". . .a responsiveness rich in creative initiative is eminently compatible with the charismatic nature of the Religious Life." Some of the qualities we need to dream a different future are clearly enumerated here: initiative, creativity and holiness, with courage and a capacity for enterprise as motivating qualities.

The future of Religious Life is not for us to invent—that is a divine prerogative—but one we can anticipate co-creatively. We do so by befriending in a more discerning way the decline and death of the old model, by courageous risk-taking with new experiments, and by embracing with deeper wisdom and insight the new world order struggling to unfold all around us. Allegiance to the past is not the primary quality for this time. In evolutionary terms we are always building on the past, but the successful negotiation of the transition is much more about heeding the allurement of the future rather than clinging tenaciously to what we feel sure about. That desire for certainty is a feature of human insecurity; this is what often inhibits us from risking all for the sake of the Kingdom of God.

Current developments in the physical and social sciences indicate more clearly what future strands of evolutionary development will look like. These are helpful indicators—pointers to the new paradigm—as we strive to read the signs of the times and respond more creatively to what our co-creative God is begetting at this time. The following are some of the significant features:

1. The New Cosmology highlights a growing sense of convergence and connectedness among elements of creation that we have tended to perceive in a separated and atomistic way. Commonalities rather than differences will be significant for the future.

2. The human rational way of discerning and understanding life is seriously deficient. The intuitive and imaginative faculties need to be reclaimed and rehabilitated in both our spiritual and political discernments.

3. All forms of patriarchal governance tend to become dysfunctional and corrupt. The culture of organic networking offers much more hope for the future.

4. The patriarchal philosophy of divide and conquer has grown weary and cumbersome. Although the dominant culture will cling on defensively, we need to find ways to distance ourselves from its influence.

5. Care for our earth is not some esoteric new-age notion. It is probably the single greatest moral imperative of our time.

6. The Capitalistic ideology of consumerism and competition is highly destructive and is definitely not of God. We need to abandon it and embrace more egalitarian and cooperative ways of engaging with cosmic and planetary life.

7. Ours is a world bombarded with man-made information much of which is superficial and some of which is potentially destructive. What we need is a wisdom that embraces deeper and more enduring values.

8. Systemic violence is one of the biggest challenges of our age. It reaps havoc on people and habitat alike. Most of the meaningless violence is human-induced and thus becomes the single greatest challenge to humanity if we stand any hope of surviving meaningfully upon the earth.

9. All the religions have become enmeshed in patriarchal power-games. There is an urgent need to embrace afresh the more liberating spirituality of pre-religious times.

10. From a developmental perspective, the human species is called to outgrow the adolescent-type codependence that characterizes patriarchal governance, and to embrace authentic adulthood in our human and planetary relations.

Only after we have read the signs of our times with depth and breadth of vision will we be receptive for God's new dream for the vowed life. Then founding people are likely to be called forth anew and then a

fresh paradigm congruent to meet the new needs will
begin to take shape. In its major expressions, the refounding of Religious Life will be totally new. It will
embrace the urgent needs of our time and our future,
and not the specific needs of a bygone age. And if older
Religious families are to survive, they will do so, as in
previous times, not by clinging on to their earlier *raison
d'etre* but by embracing the new vision. With or without us, a new paradigm will be born and the innovative Spirit will once more draw new life from the dead
bones of the old model.

PARADIGMS IN DECLINE

*The last act of a dying organization is to get out a new
and enlarged edition of the rule book.*

JOHN GARDNER

Not many years ago, the West ruled the rest of the world. The Western impact—especially through globalization—is still visibly extensive. And those who belong to the cultures of the South—Africa, Asia and Latin America—often take a distinctive pride in emulating the West. The MacDonaldization of culture may be frequently condemned, but for the rank-and-file of humanity, its benefits are alluring and appealing.

The hegemony of Western values is far more powerful and insidious than most people realize. And it is strongly reinforced by social, political and religious validation. This is the hegemony of patriarchy which, more than any other cultural artifact, resists major change. It wishes to cling on to what works, to what has stood the test of time, what helps to make money and what guarantees the unquestioned supremacy of those who believe they have the right to rule and dominate.

The Patriarchal, Imperial Tenor

This imperialistic hegemony is much more powerful than many of us would care to acknowledge. It dominates every aspect of our lives with devastating effects for the poor and marginalized which comprise at least 50% of humanity. As a social scientist, I detect a number of subtle and enduring values which the imperial culture fosters with some devious ingenuity. These include:

1. We only deal with timespans that can be measured and quantified according to the criteria of objective reason. The 2,000 year limit is singularly important and after that, the 3,500 year parameter which marks the rise of human-based civilization. Anything before those dates is of questionable worth, because it cannot be subjected to the scrutiny of objective reason.

2. Humans reflect the image and likeness of God in whom is embodied the supreme wisdom that rules the world. This entitles humans to rule as God would rule and, consequently, human perception is basically beyond error. This delusion is known as anthropocentrism, often leading humans (especially, males) to behave as if God does not exist, and in that case, they become "gods" unto themselves.

3. The ability to discern truth in a rational and objective way is a distinctive feature of civilized humans. However, men possess this capacity in a much more masterly way than women.

4. The imperial male mind-set is often described as the patriarchal way of viewing reality. It deems everything to be ordered in hierarchical fashion and validated by the divine wisdom that governs from the top of the pyramid.

5. The governance of patriarchy also requires clear-cut divisions between what can be managed in an orderly way and what cannot be. Dualistic divisions are perceived to be of God and must be upheld and protected.

Religious Life Values

As I shall indicate in the first subsection of this chapter, religion tends to espouse and reinforce the imperial value-system, despite the fact that religionists of all persuasions will question this perception. The old model of Religious Life strongly embraces such values:

a) Unquestioned allegiance to the Ruling God (of Christendom), mediated through hierarchical leaderships.

b) Emphasis on ascetical spirituality—prayer, fasting, obedience, etc.—to placate the ever demanding, moralistic God.

c) A spiritual vision heavily imbued with dualistic divisions between this sinful world and

eternal bliss in a world beyond (the eschatological rationale).

d)   Heavy emphasis on structure and order,
     clearly articulated in Canon Law and in Con-
     stitutions derived therefrom.

e)   A strong individualistic spirituality forever try-
     ing to placate a demanding deity.

f)   Sublimation of creative energy into work and
     penance, rendering unstinting service within
     a largely anthropocentric vision, where people
     matter but not the wider creation.

The values we adopted in the past, in the name of
being set apart from the world, actually mirrored and
repeated those of the surrounding culture. They provided counter-cultural witness, not by conscious choice
but because of a deeper spiritual wisdom that characterizes the vowed life in every generation. We look back
on heroic people who did heroic deeds in an age when
heroism was a spiritual virtue. While wishing to honor
the memory of those on whose shoulders we stand, we
also know that the call of our time—and the critical
values for now—are significantly different from former
times, and call us to a different quality of response.

In Religious communities today we tend to cherish
the older traditions by retaining artifacts in libraries
and museums. We display pictures, icons, and images
of saintly people, and of outstanding achievements. We
celebrate feasts and anniversaries. We often narrate
stories, sometimes bemusingly, to both the young and

the old in our ranks. Unknowingly, we create a monu-
ment of security based on the past. Nothing is ever
allowed to die, and therefore old ideologies can easily
become a barrier to the birth of radical newness.

We often recall the past. Our problem is around
integrating it, retaining what will serve to move us on,
and shedding that which will encumber our future. We
consider the retention of the past essential for continuity. But is this God's continuity, which historically
tends to be the paradox of creation and destruction or,
in the East, the trajectory of birth-death-rebirth, or is
it a creation of our collective insecurity? A careful study
of the history of Religious Life, especially from the perspective of the great Foundresses, shows that Religious
Life thrives on risk-for-the-future rather than on securities based on the past.

These are profound questions for all of us trying to
make sense of paradigm shifts and their impact on
Religious Life today. One issue is beginning to mature
into a solid guideline for our growth and sense of direction: *In moving forward, we build on the past, but
we must also be able to travel light by shedding the
baggage that is no longer useful.* What I want to name
and identify in this Chapter are aspects of the encum-
bering baggage of the old paradigm. We cannot hope to
dispose of them until we first name them. The naming
helps to clarify the cultural context of former times
and the cultural conditioning we now need to forego if
we are to respond creatively to the new horizons that

beckon us at this time. Precious though our historical legacy may be, it must not become an obstacle to the future that lures us forth—to the new horizons where the creative Spirit blows afresh in our time.

THE FIRST LETTING-GO:
THE GOD-IMAGE OF 2000 YEARS

*The process of spiritual growth is one of deconstructing
this childish God-image and moving into adult relationship with the transcendentally immanent Holy Mystery,
who is both the ground of all being and utterly beyond
our imaging, our language, our control.*

SANDRA M. SCHNEIDERS

Building on a long spiritual and scholarly tradition,
Joan Chittister (1995, 46ff.) claims that the Religious
Life is above all else, an unambiguous assertion of the
primacy of God in human life. More than anything else,
the Religious is "intoxicated with God." And that intimate longing for the divine tends to be expressed in
nuptial imagery as brides of Christ the Bridegroom (see
VC, Nos. 33, 55, 56, 89, 92, 167, 173).

In every time and culture, our allegiance to God is
mediated through human images and perceptions the
nature of which alters with changing cultural circumstances. In the Western world, Christians traditionally
imaged God as a supreme, kingly, male figure, ruling
from above and beyond the sky. Christian catechesis
in many parts of the world seeks to convey the identity
of God as that of an earth-like father. In every age, our
faith in God is expressed and mediated through concepts and ideas loaded with human projection and
heavily colored by prevailing cultural norms.

As humans, we always need images and concepts in order to envisage the divine presence so that we can relate to it in prayer, service and relationship. Cultural accretions will always feature in our spiritual praxis. Obviously, the challenge is to keep these "externals" as transparent as possible to the ultimate mystery that evokes our allegiance and to exercise discerning responsibility on our choice of metaphors, images, concepts, and ideas.

What Christ are We Following?

For the purposes of the present essay, I want to examine one central inculturation of the Christian Jesus and its implications for Religious women and men in our following of Christ today (the *sequela Christi*). For most of the Christian era, the Churches and Christian scholarship have emphasized the uniqueness of Jesus over, and against, any other understanding of God. This has been modified somewhat as multifaith dialogue grows and develops (see Dupuis 1997; Phan 2003).

For the Christian churches, the uniqueness of Jesus hinges on the 2,000 year benchmark, an axial moment of global significance beginning in 1 AD. For many of the Christian churches, that date reconstitutes the beginning of everything else in creation. What happens before that date is deemed to be relatively unimportant compared to what happens thereafter. In Christian terms, a new age has dawned; the world has been begotten anew.

The breakthrough that occurred in 1 AD becomes more pronounced as the Christian church develops its theory of salvation, and christology effectively gives way to soteriology. Salvation is understood to have commenced with Christ about 2,000 years ago. Although the Christian church also acknowledges a salvific relationship with God in the Hebrew Scriptures (via the notion of the Covenant), that is merely an anticipation for the "real thing" that will unfold in the life and death of Christ, and will form the foundation of Christian life thereafter.

This is a subtle but very powerful benchmark that has dominated Christian belief and practice since the time of Christ, namely that the Christian era, beginning in 1 AD, is when time really begins, and God's relationship with humanity assumes radically new meaning. Prior to that time, we understood God to rule and judge from a distant heaven. Although people believed in God's providence and care, many felt alienated from God and therefore, a meaningful spiritual life was deemed to be improbable, if not totally impossible.

The God of Creation

Amazingly, Christian scholars seem reluctant to acknowledge the disturbing shortsightedness of this view and the dangerous idolatry it so quickly engenders. Every catechetical program throughout the Christian centuries begins by acknowledging that God created and sustains the world. Irrespective of whether or not we accept the notion of a Big Bang, we know that God's creation has been unfolding for *billions* of years and that God has been fully involved in the process throughout that entire time.

Consequently, the primary revelation of God to us is in the cosmic creation itself. God was revealing God's self through the unfolding of creation over several billions of years long before organic life evolved some four billion years ago, and for billions of years before humans first appeared on the scene around six million years ago.

People of our time seem to be growing weary of the reductionistic God of the past 2,000 years. As more people become aware of creation's great story, the 2,000-year-old God becomes increasingly dissatisfying both spiritually and humanly. The mysterious attractiveness of God is much more transparent and meaningful in the elegance and paradoxical nature of creation itself. And it is this God, too, that engages growing numbers of contemporary Religious (particularly women) in their prayer and spirituality and in their engagement with God's creation.

The conventional paradigm of God, focused on the 2,000 years of Christendom (or on the 3,500 years of formal religion), is rapidly losing credibility. Religious encounter this disillusionment in young and old alike. It impacts on their own spiritual growth and development. It evokes new questions that can no longer be subverted. Religious today will be satisfied with nothing less than an enlarged horizon of theological meaning.

The Incarnational Face of God

With the enlarged horizon of divine allurement comes a new search for the Christ of our Christian faith. Why confine Incarnation to a 2,000-year period when we know God was fully with us in our unfolding story of 6,000,000 years? The divine solidarity with our unfolding humanity does not begin with Jesus; more accurately, it culminates in Jesus as a supreme divine affirmation of everything we humans have achieved during that evolutionary time.

God does not become incarnate in human flesh for the first time 2,000 years ago. God has been fully, unambiguously, with humans in their evolutionary unfolding over 6,000,000 years. God's grace, salvation and empowerment has been with us the whole way, even in those dark and confusing times when we clearly did not get it right. And the historical life of Jesus, around 2,000 years ago, is better seen as an affirmation and celebration of all that we achieved over our earthbound journey, while also marking a new horizon into which evolution will lead us in the future.

Yes, this is Incarnation writ large, with the elegance and expansiveness of divine creativity. Religious, at their finest moments in history, specialize in expanding narrow and congesting horizons. This is what our liminality and prophetic witness calls us to be about.

Today, we are called not merely to expanding horizons of hope and meaning for the poor and marginalized, but also to stretch those theological boundaries which dishonor not merely human greatness but the global embrace of our creative God.

As we seek to rescue God—and Jesus—from Western imperial minimalism, all the horizons of the vowed life take on added dimensions. We begin to encounter those new horizons in Chapter Three of this book, and their fuller implications are spelt out in Chapter Four. The implications are far-reaching, and for many, deeply disturbing. But the liminal space was never intended to be a comfort zone, and if we abdicate this challenge, we betray something that belongs to the very heart of our vocation, namely our intoxication with God.

As we adopt these new theological horizons, the following are some of the new parameters we will have to negotiate in the years ahead:

1. Religious in several parts of the world have already outgrown the sacred vs. secular dualism. In the spirit of many of the great founders (more accurately, the great foundresses), they are immersed in the world at the service of the Kingdom of God.

2. Christian Religious Life is likely to outgrow its close attachment to the formal Church, which is likely to remain hidebound in its attachment to the God of the 2,000-year boundary.

3. The governing laws and guidelines for living the vowed life will tend to rely more on the call to serve

God at the heart of the world, rather than away from the world which was the focus of the earlier spirituality.

4. The perceptual identification of Religious with the priestly way of life will alter significantly as Religious themselves begin to reclaim the primacy of their lay identity.

More than anything else, it is the contemplative fascination with the cosmic creativity of God that will engage Religious of the future (see Chittister 1995; Fiand 2001; Schneiders 2001; Sammon 2002). And it is this same God-centered allurement that will compel them to be God's ambassadors at the heart of creation. To engage responsibly at that level, and honor the just yearnings of God, Religious will have to engage with political, economic and systemic forces, particularly those that undermine God's creativity in the world today. The nature of this challenge becomes clearer in subsequent chapters of this book.

Second Letting-go:
PATRIARCHAL RELIGION

Contemporary Religious Life is just now emerging from a period that has been both blessed and burdensome. Those of us who are its members continue to face some formidable and complex challenges. The work that lies ahead will require of us open minds, a willingness to surrender divisive ideological points of view, and a great deal of sacrifice.

Sean D. Sammon

Paradigm shifts vary in lengths of time, some lasting a few centuries and others extending over several millennia. The declining paradigm under review in the present section, namely patriarchy, has had a lifespan covering at least 8,000 years. Consequently, its decline is likely to be prolonged and chaotic, with no small measure of resistance from those committed to this mode of ordering and controlling reality.

Patriarchy is a loosely defined concept to denote the rule of governance, characterized by dominance and control, pioneered and facilitated primarily by men. Some scholars trace its origins to the rise of classical science in the 17th century; others, to ancient Greek principles of governance; while others, like myself, believe it is a by-product of early agricultural times when humans first systematically domesticated land and made it the basis of ownership and male privilege.

Divine Validation

In this context, the origins of patriarchy can be dated to about 8,000 BCE with its more virulent form from 5,000 BCE. Virtually all forms of governance in the modern world are patriarchal in nature, characterized by a clear line of command from the top down. The philosophy of patriarchy is a good deal more subtle, particularly its central tenet: *progress is procured by a strategy of divide and conquer and it is sustained by fidelity to the wisdom from on high mediated from God via the king, the pope, the prime minister, the executive director, superior, etc.*

Of all the leading paradigms we know today, patriarchal rule is the most widespread and culturally sanctioned. It governs and controls the sphere of politics and economics and is extensively validated by all the main religions. God is deemed to be the great patriarch, whose power is mediated downward through a series of earthly, hierarchical figures: the elite clerics of economics, science and religion. People constitute the base of the pyramid and in that capacity well over 70% of humanity feel totally disempowered regarding all the main issues that impact on their daily lives.

Politically and ecclesiastically, patriarchal governance has lost much of its meaning and credibility. Some scholars maintain that in terms of models of governance we are between paradigms, with an older authoritarian model losing relevance and a new egalitarian, participatory mode evolving in a creative and chaotic way. My personal sense is that the old model has already lost its meaning, and is in irreversible decline, despite the fact that billions cling to it in terms of external allegiance, but internally regard it with growing apathy and indifference.

This is particularly so in the sphere of religion. While millions cherish the notion of religion as a cultural acquisition, there is a noted decline in terms of practice, and among those who do, they choose what appeals and ignore what seems irrelevant. Authority from within the various religions and churches—apart from Islamic regimes—exercises diminishing influence on political, social and economic values. Meanwhile, evangelical sects thrive in many parts of the contemporary world, fuelled not by a hunger for the spiritual, but by a craving for security and clarity to cope with a world of rapid change.

Pastoral Dilemmas

For growing numbers of Religious, this creates pastoral and personal dilemmas of increasing complexity:

1. In the popular perception Religious are assumed to be in close affiliation with the hierarchical church. In their personal lives and increasingly in community discernment, allegiance to the Church is questionable, precarious and sometimes experienced as a major obstacle. As Religious befriend the people of God in a range of personal and pastoral situations, the people's spiritual questions, anxieties and concerns pose formidable challenges.

2. The search for meaning in today's world far transcends the conventional answers of formal creed
   and dogma. In exercising a discerning sensitivity,
   Religious (esp. women) increasingly find that promoting the official response of a church or a religion is evasive, lacking in discernment, and sometimes an insult to people's intelligence and integrity.

3. Growing numbers of Religious today study theology and spirituality. They are aware of the ten-
   dentious issues in Church and society. They are
   aware of the critical skills employed by Scripture
   scholars and the disturbing questions raised by
   modern theologians.

4. Because of their exposure to the rank-and-file of
   modern society, Religious are often painfully aware
   that many people will not entrust their questions
   or concerns to Religious, fearing they might ob-
   tain the rebuttal of ecclesiastical correction. Instead, people will take their concerns to someone
   outside the Church rather than to those they perceive as over-identifying with the formal ecclesiastical position.

Codependency

One of the disturbing features of patriarchal governance is the underhand manner in which people are
indoctrinated. They are encouraged not to think for
themselves and, therefore, they tend to become increasingly dependent on the wisdom of the governing group.

This easily breeds a culture of codependency in which people find it hard—nor indeed, are they encouraged—to behave like adults invoking their adult wisdom.

In a world of mass information, this situation is rapidly changing. People tend to be much more aware and informed on options and choices. Choices regarding values and lifestyle tend to be made on the weight of evidence rather than on the advice or recommendation of a higher authority. Within the Christian churches, theology, the one time monopoly of clerics, is now extensively read and studied by lay people, including several Religious women. Within the next decade, the Catholic Church will face a major challenge when the majority of its theologians will not be priests but lay people (see Chap. 3, Section One).

As people become more informed, they question and challenge the status quo. This is often dismissed or condemned as an adolescent-type rebellion. This is much more a proactive initiative based on renewed self-confidence, in a culture where more people risk evoking their adult selves. This is not so much about disobedience to an outer authority as allegiance to an inner wisdom.

And we need to be wary of those who will dismiss this newfound integrity as postmodernist individualism. This is not so much about people acting in isolation. Today, people check alternative sources of wisdom and guidance often through their affiliation to one or more supportive networks. While there is a move away from consulting those at the top, there is a growing trend in peer supervision, peer support, and group discernment.

Beyond the Culture of Denial

The closing decades of the 20th century marked a time of re-entrenchment. Right-wing governments seemed to enjoy a revival while religions and churches grew more conservative and petrified. These are predictable features when culture undergoes a paradigm shift. What we tend to underestimate is the global scale of this regressive trend and the time it will take to resolve it. We are looking at *decades* rather than *single years*. In the end the new consciousness will gain ascendancy and a new paradigm will progressively unfold.

In this realm, more than any other, Religious are called to be critically prophetic. In collaboration with the people of God, we need to name what is dying and fading into history. When and where possible we need to ritualize the dying and letting go. In our Western culture, heavily addicted to denial, we need to seize every opportunity to help people grapple with what is *really* happening. Consequently, we need to invoke and affirm the use of imagination, creative dialogue, exploratory networking, and the courage to engage in liberating rituals.

To that end we need to be vigilant about the language we use to describe and explore our understanding of Religious Life. The notion that ours is a *conse-*

crated form of life has been much in vogue since the early 1990s. It is strongly endorsed in the Catholic document, *Vita Consecrata*. Within the Catholic hierarchy, one finds a widespread view that Religious Life today is in crisis because Religious are lacking in holiness, sanctity and prayer. Therefore, they need to reclaim the special nature of their consecration to God. And although that consecration is understood to be a deeper living of the Baptismal consecration shared by all Christians, in the case of Religious, it is considered somehow better than that commonly espoused by Christians in general.

This is a regression to the Pre-Vatican Two spirituality of the vowed life, when Religious Life was perceived to be a better, holier and more authentic way of serving God. That understanding can be traced back to the Council of Trent when the priest alone was deemed to be the only fully fledged Christian; Religious came next and lay people were at the base of the ladder leading to holiness. Vatican Two tried to reclaim the universal call to holiness, open to all God's people and lived out in a complementary (not hierarchical) set of vocational options. According to *Lumen Gentium* (32): "All are called to holiness and have obtained an equal privilege of faith through the justice of God." And the document goes on to assert, "It is therefore quite clear that all Christians in whatever state or walk in life are called to the fullness of Christian life and to the perfection of charity" (40).

The recent emphasis on consecration carries the risk of reassigning Religious Life to the closet of perfectionism. A tiered class system of being righteous before God is being invoked once more. The rhetoric of fleeing the world and transcending the body is likely to assume new meaning. All these developments militate seriously against the liminal and prophetic nature of the vowed life and will do little towards a mutual enrichment of vocational options for the good of the whole Church.

As a social scientist, I also detect in this emphasis, a movement towards a more introverted spirituality, a desire to gain more control over Religious women and men. The controlling clout of patriarchal power is surfacing once more, cleverly validated by a kind of religious rhetoric that cuts little ice in the modern world. There is a desire on the part of the hierarchical church to relocate the vowed life in the enclosure of consecration. We are perceived to be a threat to, or a distraction from, the formal organization of the Church. This rather functionalist view, apart from being ecclesially defective, also shows a very poor understanding of the theological meaning of Religious Life.

Third Letting-go:
THE POWER OF DUALISMS

*I wish to take incarnation seriously; and this is not pos-
sible through the veil of Greek metaphysics. Therefore,
we have to get brutal with metaphysics.*

LISA ISHERWOOD

Every religion gives priority to the sacred over the
secular. The former is deemed to be of God and important for our salvation; the latter is contrary to God and
endangers our immortal future.

All dualisms start from a foundational conviction
that God inhabits a non-material, heavenly realm, imbued with the Spirit of holiness. Everything else, and
especially the sphere of material creation, is somehow
alien to God and a distraction from following Christ in
a God-like way.

The False Neatness

Dualisms are essentially figments of the patriarchal imagination, crystallized in the binary
conceptualizations of classical Greek thought. They
reinforce the patriarchal desire to divide and conquer
by setting everything in an adversarial relationship. Life
comes to be understood as an unending contest between good and evil. Everything in creation is catego-
rized to be on one side or the other; the ancient Greeks

were particularly fond of such divisive strategies. Redemptive violence thrives on this division.

The dualistic worldview is about human manipulation rather than divine grace. Dualisms are grossly simplistic and fail to honor the paradoxical evolutionary nature of divine co-creativity in the world. These simple binary distinctions distract from the complex mystery through which our God makes all things new. Our world is created in freedom and the pathway of cosmic and planetary evolution is marked by success and failure, by breakthrough and breakdown, by creation and destruction (See Swimme & Berry 1992; O'Murchu 2002). However, the providential nature of unconditional love guarantees an eventual outcome in which goodness triumphs—not in spite of darkness and chaos but actually through those disintegrating forces. Pitching that which is constructive in dualistic opposition to that which is destructive will never enable us to resolve or befriend the paradox on which creation thrives.

The dualistic division is born of the human mind, unable to comprehend and honor the binary polarities of God's creation. For God, it is always "both-and," never "either-or." The divine embrace honors the complexities, paradoxes and even the contradictions of evolution's course. Humans like neat manageable packages. They may be neat, but they are not real.

The Monastery vs. the World

The prevailing theology of Religious Life is heavily infiltrated with dualistic divisions, the most basic being that of the monastery vs. the world. This has often led to an escapist spirituality largely devoid of incarnational meaning. For much of the early Benedictine epoch—right up to the 10th century—the monastic vision transcended this dualistic divide, making a major contribution to the commercial, agricultural and intellectual development of the European landmass. Today, the dualistic distinctions tend to feature in the Eastern rather than in the Western monastic systems.

Closer to our own time, especially in the 1700's and 1800's, we note the binary undercurrents in the Jansenistic worldview, preoccupied with the salvation of one's soul, while failing to address the widespread exploitation of God's creation. Despite this narrow, anti-world spirituality, Religious women and men pioneered several courageous endeavors for the education and medical well-being of the poor and marginalized in society. With the contemporary emphasis on *consecration* we are in danger once more of creating divisive, dualistic barriers.

Nowhere was the dualistic influence more damaging than in dealing with the human body and its creative potentials. Our human-embodied condition is precisely where our incarnational God is most at home. Yet, we have demonized and dishonored the body, leaving us with a tragic travail of brokenness, pain and unworthiness. Millions of people today do not feel at home in their bodies—including many Religious women and men—and are unable to praise and thank God for their embodied giftedness.

The disembodiment perpetuated by religion has also quite seriously undermined the sacred nature of human sexuality. For many Religious, celibate commitment may be a sign of holiness but it is questionable whether it contributes to incarnational wholesomeness. Sexuality was split off, rather than integrated, and that which is split off is likely to haunt us, which may well be what was happening in the sexual abuse cases that came to light in the closing decades of the 20th century.

Our desexualized and disembodied spirituality also reinforced our emotional and spiritual distance from God. The Divine was perceived to be in his heaven, safely ensconced from the sinful erotic world. How quickly we seem to forget that the creative energy we describe as erotic is none other than God's own capacity for birthing forth new life in the wonders of cosmic and planetary creation. Dualisms cut deeply—into the human, the planetary, the cosmic, and even into the divine creativity itself. How do we restore the unity and make whole once more that which we have so brutally fragmented?

The Ministry of Befriending

As Religious today try to face the call to become prophetic catalysts in the world, many still struggle to outgrow the irrational fear that they might be contaminated by the world and end up being unfaithful to God. The dualistic bind has de-energized us and, at times distracted us from the liminal task to which we are called.

The spirituality of divisiveness needs to be replaced by a spirituality of befriending. Just as our God befriends creation—in its unfolding process of light and shadow—so we, too, are called to befriend what God has entrusted to our care. Several dimensions are embraced in this inclusive vision:

a) We are called to befriend cosmic creation as God's primary revelation to us, the oldest and most enduring expression of the divine creativity.

b) We are called to befriend our earthiness, the planetary grounding that generates and sustains human living on a daily basis.

c) We are called to befriend the vast array of living organisms without which we could not live meaningful lives.

d) We are called to befriend our embodied selves so that we may utilize with maximum creativity the giftedness that empowers us for the service of mission.

e) We are called to befriend every aspect of creation in the direction of justice so that the abundant gift of life can be enjoyed by all, especially the poor and marginalized.

Befriending is a caring stance with unique possibilities. It transcends the compulsive desire for control so central to patriarchal domination. It also transcends the well-intentioned patronizing often adopted in the parenting mode. Befriending acknowledges the right of the other as *other* in both its strengths and vulnerabilities. It does not stand in judgment over what is acceptable as distinct from what is unacceptable. It seeks to work with the whole, not with the divided reality.

Liminal Bridge-Building

Religious Life witness focuses on a world made new. It seeks to foster fidelity to the God who unites rather than divides, within a spirituality that makes whole rather than fragments. And it casts the net of healing and inclusiveness across the whole of God's creation from the cosmos to the person. What splits the one splits everything; what heals the one helps eventually to bring forth universal peace.

This counter-cultural stance is explored in Chapter Four under the rubric of *liminality*. This anthropological concept helps to give contemporary expression to the Biblical call to be in the world but not of it. This is a very different quality of presence from the divisive one invoked in the name of anti-world dualisms. Religious belong unambiguously to the realm of God's creation in its total cosmic and planetary context. Precisely because of this total presence to, and deep love for, God's creation, the vowed Religious are called to question, denounce, and challenge all those values which contravene or undermine the primacy of the divine at work in creation.

Contrary to dualistic engagement, with its either-or options, Religious seek to serve as bridge-builders, healing the rifts that tear people apart, that exploit the God-given resources of the planet and that trivialize the divine by restricting its primary influence to the transcendent heavenly realm. In a world where so much "dis-membering" has taken place, often fuelled by religion, Religious embrace "re-membering" as one of the most urgent pastoral and political tasks of our time.

From the liminal space apart, Religious women and men see the bigger and deeper picture. While total immersion in the world can exhaust the energy that needs to be mobilized for the contemplative gaze, over-identifying with one half of the binary divide will undermine our ability to discern what God desires to be embraced with Gospel compassion and love. The Religious is in the world, and yet can serve it well by holding in the liminal space, the ambiguity and ambivalence which feeds the paradox and inexplicable nature of the enduring mystery.

Fourth Letting-go:
ECCLESIASTICAL, CANONICAL CONTROL

Today we are experiencing a worldwide institutional cri-
sis where the old religious sanctions and admonitions
are simply exhausted. Nobody listens to them anymore.
IVONE GEBARA

After his return from the Second Vatican Council
in 1963, the then auxiliary Bishop of London (UK), B.C.
Butler, OSB, wrote these words:

But few of us seemed to have very clear or distinct
ideas about the theology of Religious Life; or if we did
they proved singularly out of harmony with the general
theological renewal that was taking shape within the
Council itself. In default of a good and dynamic theol-
ogy our temptation seemed to be to take refuge behind
the bastions of Canon Law.

Few people have named our theological dilemma so
strongly and succinctly. Even at the beginning of the
21st century, we, Religious, lack a theology that can
situate and sustain our vowed life where it primarily
belongs: in the world at the service of the Kingdom of
God. Two ideologies get in the way: the first is an insipid type of spiritualism, couched afresh under the
rubric of consecration; the second, a destructive type
of legalism whereby we feel that in following the law

(Constitutions), all is well between us and God. While neither obstacle is consciously espoused, together they exert a crippling impact on our diminished sense of theological vision.

Ecclesiastical Control

Ever since the Council of Trent in the 16th century, Religious Life has been viewed as a maverick movement that needs to be kept under the firm hand of ecclesiastical control. Because of its essentially prophetic nature it is endemic to Religious Life to push boundaries, to challenge existing systems, to dream new visions for both Church and world. Failure to do so would be an abdication of our uniqueness as a counter-cultural movement.

Situating the vowed life in a definitive legal framework of the institutional Church diminishes not only Religious Life itself, but also the Church in which it is called to be a prophetic presence. The compulsion for control condemns Religious Life to a type of lowest-common-denominator, stripped of any real capacity for bold and original witness. All too easily we can end up with another dualism where the institutional church is the active controlling agent, while Religious Life becomes a type of passive organism. This contradicts even the basic meaning of law as a force for the preservation of liberating freedom.

However, the creative Spirit is not easily muted. Despite prohibitions that hinder radical presence, Religious, in many situations, find ways to circumvent the barrier of prohibitive law. In the pastoral sphere, we speak to the heart rather than to the head. Our responses are often governed by the immediacy of need, and the compassion it calls forth in us there and then. As Religious we tend to be at our best in serving God's people, and our charismatic gifts flourish best when we remain close to our people. At that level we transcend the legalism which all too often is associated with the Church and its governance. We witness to the human face of our God—compassionate, healing and always seeking to make whole.

Beyond Clericalism

Perhaps, the greatest damage to our uniqueness as Religious was the superior status attributed to the priest after the Council of Trent in the 16th century. Thereafter, the priest alone was considered to be the Christian par excellence and all other vocations had to be modeled on that of the priest. Therefore, all Religious—Sisters, Brothers and Priests—were considered in terms of the Tridentine template even down to the details of sisters and brothers obliged to wear a form of dress emulating the basic black and white of the clerical outfit.

Religious were to behave like clerics, pray like clerics and function according to clerical norms. Moreover, they had to be responsible to clerics, not just for ecclesiastical accountability, but also for guidance in their spiritual formation. The calling to Religious Life became a subservient type of vocation governed essentially by the same laws and procedures as those of clerical priesthood.

So, too, at the ministerial level. Service to the people of God was construed in terms of administration of sacraments over which the priest had a monopoly. Sisters and Brothers teaching in schools were assumed to be preparing youth for a life in the Church. Religious working in hospitals were expected to follow the moral and pastoral guidelines adopted by the clericalized Church. The much more radical service, rendered by female Religious particularly, was often subverted and not accorded due historical recognition even to the present time.

This clerical monopoly of all Christian life ultimately reaped its own destruction. Even the Catholic Church itself recognized the undesirable imbalance and at the Second Vatican Council initiated a shift in our understanding of the basic call to holiness. This call is extended to all Christians, equally shared in our common baptism, uniquely experienced in the lay, Religious and clerical states, and not just the reserve of one select group.

Although the shift has been named and, today, spiritual growth is being facilitated by people of many different backgrounds, the clericalized monopoly, with its legal and institutional baggage, still exerts a great deal of influence. Our understanding of the vows is still largely one of legal observance and prohibition, despite several alternative interpretations explored by scholars over the past twenty years (see the useful resume of Leonard 2002). Membership of Orders and Congregations tends to be defined in ecclesiastical terms despite the fact that the emerging theology of Religious Life focuses unambiguously on the priority of the Kingdom of God.

Shifting Allegiance

The old paradigm lingers on, sometimes with an uncompromising stubbornness, but in the hearts and minds of Religious across the globe, the allegiance is shifting as many within and without the vowed life question the basic meaning of the existing paradigm. The credibility of those who govern from on high has been seriously dented in recent decades. This has happened politically, socially and religiously. Precisely because Religious tend to be close to the ordinary people, knowing more experientially their struggles and hopes, Religious too begin to identify with their disillusionment and desire for change.

Religious Life itself is engulfed in the same structural crisis that affects governance at every level of contemporary life: we no longer trust the wisdom from on high, especially the imposed wisdom. We seek more egalitarian, dialogical ways to discern the call to service in the church and world of our time. We desire greater transparency within and outside our ranks. We wish to be treated as adults, invited to engage in creating the laws and guidelines that will affect our lives rather than inheriting them from what growing numbers among us regard as an outdated parental monopoly.

This is not some type of postmodern adolescent rebellion. As Religious committed to the *sequela Christi* we are called to grow into the full stature of Christ in our fidelity to the mission of the Kingdom of God. This, too, is the mission to which the whole Church is called, but for Religious, the building up of God's Kingdom in the world carries a greater urgency.

The Religious Life is older than Church or formal religion. It belongs to that cutting-edge consciousness (liminality) whereby humans call forth some of their own members to serve as a prophetic vanguard. People have done this from time immemorial, and apparently always will—whether the Church lives or dies. Perhaps this is the most salient, yet most powerful motive inviting Religious today into a new paradigm to honor their call and mission as a universal empowering force.

FIFTH LETTING-GO:
PREOCCUPATION WITH THE SINFUL WORLD

A great deal of Christian talk has been sin-obsessed. The distortion has been appalling.

NORMAN PITTENGER

Between the years 2001 and 2003, the three-part movie, *Lord of the Rings*, was viewed on the big screen in many countries worldwide. The story is that of a contemporary mythic tale in pursuit of an ultimate Kingdom which is attained at the end of Part Three of the movie. But the journey to that ultimate goal is haunted by the unrelenting battle of "good vs. evil." Cultural decadence, human violence, and extreme destruction of habitat feature strongly in the entire movie. Despite its immense popularity among film viewers, *Lord of the Rings* is saturated with a great deal of goring violence.

The Flawed Creation

That the world is a sinful, impermanent and destructive place is an old spirituality revived with telling assertiveness in *Lord of the Rings*. The old paradigm may sound archaic and irrelevant for modern sensitivities, but the contemporary imagination, even for young people, seems to have little difficulty in entertaining its gruesome and bizarre nature. As long as the violence is converted into entertainment, then we can continue to perpetuate the age-old myth of the world being essentially a bad place. The entertainment then becomes the excuse by which we do not have to take the violence seriously, see it for what it really is as a human imposition, and mobilize our efforts to reduce its impact by creating a more just and caring world.

This same negative, world-denouncing spirituality is what nourished and sustained the vowed life particularly since the Council of Trent in the 16th century. The constitutions of orders and congregations liberally used the idea of turning one's back on the world which was regarded as a hopelessly flawed and corrupt place. God's creation was depicted as a "vale of tears," a sojourn to be endured until, in death, we escaped into the realm of lasting happiness. Ironically the negative spirituality which so influenced devotion and the inner sphere of the spiritual life, did not inhibit Religious (particularly Sisters and Brothers) from rendering generous service in building up God's Kingdom in several spheres of public and secular life.

Despite the elegance of God at work in creation, lauded in the Psalms and in the religious literature of other faith traditions, creation-based spirituality rarely entered either the consciousness or vocabulary of Religious Life. So pervasive was the negative renunciation that the Cistercians in the 12th century created a new category of membership, namely, lay-brothers, to attend to the cultivation of the land while the other monks gave their full attention to "the things of God." Here we see at work the dualistic divisions reviewed in the previous section.

The ultimate justification for this other-worldly stance was, and continues to be, the notion of Original Sin. This is considered to be the root of humankind's innate state of corruption inherited biologically from the defiant and sinful Adam. Today, the mythic tale upon which the doctrine is founded—that of rebellious angels expelled from paradise—has lost a great deal of credibility. What tragically endures however, is the accompanying anthropocentric projection: humans are born sinful, so is the whole of creation. If we are defective, creation must also be. And only a redemptive act of God, with Jesus as the supreme patriarchal scapegoat, can rescue us from the hopeless plight in which we find ourselves.[3]

Spiritual Schizophrenia

Fortunately, this stultifying spirituality did not inhibit Religious in their unstinting service to humanity, especially to the poor and marginalized of the world. Religious often excelled in helping lay people integrate their service of God and their service of creation into one spiritual and theological synthesis. Ironically, it was in their own spiritual lives that Religious often felt a kind of internal schizophrenia between their desire not to be too immersed in the world, and their deeper yearning to bridge the chasm between faith and culture.

Today, such a negative spirituality is either ignored or surpassed. Informed Christians intuit that something is amiss in this view of God and God's creation. In the past, arduous asceticism may have created heroic saintly people, even to the point of martyrdom, but several suspect that this has done little to rid the world of meaningless suffering. Some theologians question the Atonement doctrines upon which humans have erected a spurious theory of redemption. The Jesus who was radically committed to the fullness of life seems to have been sidetracked by the heroic Jesus who had to sacrifice his life to appease an offended deity, but to many thinking people, that offended deity resembles a patriarchal overlord rather than the Jesus of incarnational possibilities (cf. Brock 1992; Green & Baker 2000).

An Alternative Vision

For many people of our time, and for Religious in particular, the call to reduce meaningless suffering in the world requires a different vision and alternative strategies based on non-violence. A different quality of logic informs the contemporary imagination with the following insights to the fore:

1. God's creation is fundamentally good, endowed though it is with the paradox of creation and destruction.

2. Humans were born as people of God, beneficiaries of an original blessing rather than victims of an original sin.

3. For most of our time on earth (some 6,000,000 years) humans behaved creatively rather than sinfully, precisely because we remained very close to creation.

4. When we began to break away from the context of creation and set ourselves over against it, with the onset of patriarchal domination some 8,000 years ago, then meaningless suffering became a dominant feature of our existence.

5. Meaningless suffering, therefore, is a human, and not a divine problem. The life and death of Jesus is salvific as a prescription on how we can get back on course, rather than a remedy for a fundamental flaw that was there from the dawn of time.

6. The right relationships which Jesus has modeled for us in his life and death provide the wisdom we need to live redemptively.

7. Justice making and non-violence are the central features of a redemptively informed response.

The major problem facing Religious in trying to activate this counter-cultural approach to issues of sin and the defective worldly condition, is subtle and disturbingly convoluted. To justify their own existence, and enforce a desirable quality of control, patriarchal institutions require that earthly and human affairs are seen as basically flawed. Healthcare is a pertinent example: a) Nature provides several remedies for human pain and sickness, exemplified in the fact that most drugs are manufactured from natural resources; b) Humans are inwardly resourced to live in health rather than in sickness—as exemplified by several complementary therapies. However, if the medical profession is to remain in business, a certain proportion of people must be sick all the time, and our patriarchal codependent culture makes sure that that is the situation. A similar logic can be pursued to highlight our dysfunctional relationship with nature and, indeed, with the whole of creation.

I offer this controversial example—one that will seem farfetched and bizarre to several readers—because these are the kind of issues that Religious, true to their prophetic calling, need to name and address. While humanity turns its back on these weighty issues then the flawed sinful condition will continue to overwhelm and alienate us. But, in truth, it is we ourselves who have created the alienation, and so it is up to us to remedy the problem. And the challenge is one of working for the just and right relationships for which Jesus is our primary prophetic model.

The challenge of our time in a world saturated in meaningless violence is not to pursue peace through solidarity with suffering, but rather to do everything in our power to get rid of suffering. That quality of suffering which is innate to creation, and its evolutionary unfolding, is not the source or cause of our meaningless suffering; that is a human problem not an earthly, cosmic or divine one. That is a patriarchal problem whereby we have become alienated from creation because we have set out to conquer and control it. When we choose to withdraw our domineering projections and learn to befriend the creation that has befriended us for many millions of years then we will be able to discern the true cause of suffering in our world.

It is probably the single biggest challenge invoking the prophetic witness of Religious Life today.

SIXTH LETTING-GO:
THE SOUL OVER THE BODY

Often the wisdom of the body clarifies the despair of the spirit.

MARION WOODMAN

Just as the world (especially the earth) was spiritually suspect, so the body, too, was deemed to be an obstacle to holiness and salvation. The body was ordered and dominated by instinctual forces considered not to be of God. Within the body was an immortal soul. This was a sign of God's unique claim on an individual's life. It was the soul that gave life to the body and at death the *soul* alone would endure for life eternal.

Our Corrupt Anthropology

Anthropology is the crucial issue here. More accurately, an anthropological paradigm that has long outlived either its meaning or usefulness. Humans are portrayed as atomized units; just as the atom stands alone, so does each individual person. To bring the atomized individual alive in a real way, God infuses each organism with an immortal soul. Each soul is unique just as each individual is unique. And at death, each person will be called to render an account to God for the state of one's respective soul.

There is also an anthropological corollary. Humans are perceived to be a superior species; they alone possess souls. On the hierarchical scale of the created order, humans hold a more exalted place than any other creature. This entitles humans to act on behalf of God in mastering and using the resources of creation.

This inflated anthropology is becoming something of a nightmare for the human species today. It both sanctions and affirms our right to manipulate and exploit creation—primarily to our own benefit. This has ensued in a growing alienation from creation, leaving well over half our species impoverished, exploited and in many cases grossly abused. What we have construed to be a divinely validated right to dominance is patently becoming a form of godless exploitation.

De-souling our Arrogance

The concept of the soul, and the notion of the body needing to be ensouled by some type of direct intervention by God, needs radical reassessment. Anthropology today points us in a different direction, one that views the human person not as an isolated entity, but as an organism-in-relationship. We each belong to the web of creation, and our materialization as embodied creatures of the Planet and the Cosmos is the fruit of complex interrelated dynamics, much better understood in our time, thanks to the growing discoveries of modern science.

The following broad principles help to lead us to a

more congruent and wholesome meaning of our human soulfulness:

1. Our human becoming is not just a direct intervention of God; we are each begotten by the creative universe itself.

2. Our ensoulment is the fruit of creation's own evolutionary fertility.

3. We, like all living organisms, grow in complexity as we evolve over time.

4. Our salvation happens through our commitment to co-creation and not just through personal achievements, separate from, or in conflict with, the larger creation.

5. The dualistic split between soul and body is an aberration of God's gift of embodiment through which all spiritual growth and development takes place.

6. The priority of the soul over the body is based on an anthropocentric delusion in which humans seek to set themselves over everything else in creation and arrogantly regard themselves as the only creatures capable of being saved in eternal life.

Soulfulness

Contemporary spirituality offers an alternative way for viewing the body-soul relationship. Instead of our preoccupation with the soul within the body, we are invited to engage with the notion of the body within the soul. God's primary embodied presence in creation is in the cosmos itself, ensouled with the creative energy of God's Holy Spirit. That same inspired life-force imbues the creation and evolution of our home planet at every stage of its coming into being. And long before humans evolved, some 6,000,000 years ago, the planet was populated with bacteria whose intelligent, creative behavior has only been understood in recent decades and clearly witnesses to a soul-filled vitality.

For these various expressions and manifestations of the divine creativity at work in creation, modern writers adopt the notion of *soulfulness* (see the pioneering work of Moore 1992, 1994, 2003). Instead of reserving the holy to a spiritualized realm within the human body alone, we are invited to contemplate the holy in all that has been born of, and touched by, the living spirit of God. Instead of identifying spirituality with the soul that can transcend the body, the earth, and all created things, we are invited to engage gracefully with the holy that is immanent in the whole of creation. Instead of identifying salvation with the soul inhabiting the heavenly realm, we are invited to work together for the soulful liberation of all who live on this earth burdened with the injustice of man-made oppression.

While soul, in the conventional understanding, denotes sinlessness, purity, perfection, and transcendence of all earthly conditions, soulfulness is about "…soupy moods, impossible relationships and obsessive preoccupations" (Moore 1994, 258). We seek the sacred within the ordinary, the compassionate God who speaks through our brokenness, vulnerability, sinfulness, and even through our resistances.

Soulfulness is that wisdom through which we try to listen to the deep messages of our own bodies and the earth-body. Even our pathologies can teach us about the deep yearnings of the heart, and the complexity that sometimes haunts us because we are primed to engage with mystery. What is really inimical to soul is the literalism which dissects complexity, the fundamentalism that cannot respect pluralism, the moralism that petrifies the imagination, the perfectionism that breeds fanaticism, and the compulsion that requires a precise answer to every human dilemma.

The language of soulfulness speaks to the deeper hungers of our times. "Bringing Soul into Politics," "Soul in our Relationships," "The Soul of Science," " Soul and Spirituality," are among some of the popular book headings and conference titles of our time. While the old use of the word seems to be eroding tangible connections with the sacred, the new language evokes a spiritual desire to rediscover meaning in the ordinary experiences of daily life. Spirituality is not being abandoned or undermined; its focus is being transformed.

Religious and the Spiritual Life

For much of the Christian era, spirituality and the spiritual life were considered to be the reserve of Priests and Religious. Today, that monopoly is being challenged and transcended. The call to holiness is a universal call, not merely in terms of Christian Baptism, but by virtue of our mutual participation in the unfolding of God's creation. The call to Religious today is to be the catalysts who break open the abundant and prodigious plenitude of the Spirit in every soul and in the heart of creation itself; to call us back to that which we have neglected because we thought it was beyond our resources.

The call to perfection today is not about an exclusive focus on individual salvation but a call to honor the completeness (*pleroma*) through which God instills a living soulfulness into everything that is born from the breathing forth of the creative Spirit. Soulfulness is first and foremost an endowment of creation, inherited by all who inhabit the universe. Relocating the call to spirituality where it primarily belongs is another prophetic challenge for Religious in our time.

Seventh Letting-Go:
OBEDIENCE UNTO DEATH

In the last few centuries, Catholic life has been ravaged by the requirements of absolute obedience. . . . The theological virtues are no longer faith, hope, and charity, but submission, submission, submission.

MARK D. JORDAN

The folklore of Religious Life is richly imbued with heroic deeds of penance and self-sacrifice. Ascetical self-discipline involving fasting, prolonged prayer and denial of one's will hold an honored place in the history of Christian spirituality. The justification for such deeds of self-immolation frequently was that of mastering the rebellious passions, particularly pride. Humility became the key virtue to be nourished and cultivated.

This ascetical vein of Christian spirituality is quite a complex phenomenon. Feminist theologians question its psychological undergirding, suggesting that the battle to overcome pride is a distinctive male preoccupation. What women often need to cultivate is precisely a sense of pride in their own self-worth, since patriarchal culture has seriously undermined their legitimate sense of self-value and personal integrity.

The Rhetoric of Sacrifice

This feminist critique begs deeper questions. Is the entire ascetical endeavor a patriarchal ploy to evoke subservience and to reinforce control? The concept of sacrifice in several ancient cultures implies the pacifying and supplication of a higher (sometimes, angry) authority—divine or human. The text frequently cited, that of Abraham being asked to sacrifice his son (Gen.22:1-14) illustrates the uncompromising right of the higher authority to demand even human sacrifice. We know in several ancient (and some modern) cultures that females were often sacrificed, but that rarely gets formal or public attention. Because, it is the woman's well-being that is at stake, there is a sinister sense in which it does not matter that much. Not surprising, therefore, in the Abraham story, the boy's mother is never consulted; the story is told as if she did not exist.

The American theologian, Mary Daly, gets to the heart of the matter when she reminds us that *women shed blood in order to give life*; men shed blood in taking away life. Underlying so much of the rhetoric about sacrifice—whether in the Christian scriptures or in other faith traditions—is a covert violence that clearly is not, and cannot, be of God. Violence always begets violence and rarely leads to a creative or peaceful outcome. Violence is the opposite of the fullness of life to which Jesus calls all Christians.

The ascetical paradigm—with the emphasis on self-denial and abnegation—is a cultural phenomenon largely derived from the cult of patriarchal control. Properly understood, it has little, if anything, to do with the following of Christ. In fact, one could argue that it is quite alien to the Christian Gospel which always puts self-denial at the service of love and justice.

From earliest times, obedience becomes part of the vocabulary of asceticism. Here, *obedience* denotes subjugation to the will of another, a very different meaning from the etymology of the word which means "to listen attentively" (from the Latin *ob-audiere*). Obedience in its true Biblical sense is not about subjecting one's will to another, but utilizing all our God-given resources to listen more deeply to divine wisdom, so that we can discern God's will more authentically—for ourselves and for God's creation.

Asceticism at the Service of Mission

The ascetical orientation has fallen into disrepute, and today its practice is largely reserved to Christian sects and cults which tend to adopt a strong anti-world orientation, and a strong attachment to a punitive, judgmental God. In Christian Religious Life, ascetical devotion is largely a personal prerogative, while the collective expression veers more in the direction of giving ourselves as fully as possible to the call of mission, namely the building-up of God's Kingdom through right relationships that beget justice, love, compassion and liberation.

Instead of embracing ascetical suffering as a value in itself, we embrace the daily sufferings and sacrifices that come our way as we commit ourselves more deeply to the call to be justice-makers. We will be misunderstood, rebuffed and, at times, persecuted. We may even be rejected by the very people for whose freedom and dignity we sacrificed so much. Just as the enterprise of the Kingdom was for Jesus, so it will be for us today an undertaking that may cost us our very lives.

In this context, obedience can mean many things. It is a call to fidelity and loyalty, firstly to the creative God who invites us all to be co-creators in building a better world for all organic life. Secondly, from a Christian perspective, it is a liberating call to justice through which Jesus desires all to be free from bondage and slavery of any type. It is a call of fidelity to the entire Christian Church, as base communities of God's people seek to follow more fully the call to Christian discipleship.

In this variegated context, obedience as attentive listening, as mutual discernment, assumes central importance. It is a call to discernment over which no one authority has a monopoly. While leadership, within a universal or local church has a designated role and responsibility, those holding office do not have a monopoly over the Holy Spirit. As we embrace the complexities of modern life, discernment is likely to be more authentic when it is based on a collaborative endeavor.

For Religious in the Catholic tradition, this raises

many painful questions. Over the past thirty years we have evidenced a Church, open and receptive within the context of Vatican Two, progressively succumbing to fear, manipulation and a compulsion for control. That saddens many of us and we struggle to remain faithful in a Church that often gives the impression of not welcoming either our persons or our giftedness. Even many among us live with a fear of expressing those concerns lest we too will be victimized. The old culture of blind obedience seems to be in vogue once more, with the oppression and unhealthy phobias it inevitably invites.

The Obedient Adult

For Religious women and men in this painful situation, we have a prophetic duty to honor the adult in ourselves, in each other, and in the leadership of the Church to which we belong. In this context, our obedience is for life and not for death. Our fidelity is primarily to the one who calls us to follow in pursuing and promoting the fullness of life (Jn 10:10). And the Church to which we belong is a community of adult disciples, called into being to work collaboratively for the sake of the Kingdom. There is no room here for childish co-dependency. Adult interdependence is the procedure we have inherited from God's creation, and that is the process we should neither abdicate nor compromise.

In humility we also need to embrace those aspects of our painful past where people were hurt, damaged and alienated because of the impositions of blind obedience. The rhetoric of power has cut deep wounds in many of God's people, including those in the vowed life. Seeking healing and wholeness, many left their Orders and Congregations, convinced that their hopes to reclaim their adult selves could never be realized from within. The vow of obedience, more than any other, has left several scars in the hearts and lives of Religious women and men.

Religious of the future will need to embrace the obedient adult. This is the obedience of wisdom and care, with a healthy capacity to criticize and energize, and a deep commitment to discern collaboratively so that the giftedness of all God's people will be mobilized for the common good. A breakthrough in this complex and troubled space would really be a breadth of fresh air for the future renewal of Religious Life.

3

PARADIGMS IN TRANSITION

Nothing from the past is secure. Nothing in the future is clear. Risk is the new asceticism of Religious Life.
JOAN CHITTISTER

When we review the big picture of cosmic, planetary and human evolution, one wonders how humans could have become so attached to stability, conformity, and rigid ways of behaving and relating. Throughout the vast aeons of time, creation thrives on change, growth and development. Balance and stasis always spell stagnation. Growth and progress require fluidity, change, paradox and chaos.

A homely example is that of the human body. Every cell in the human body is replaced every seven years. There is never a time in which the process of Birth-Death-Rebirth is not at work in our bodies—as well as in our world. Transition is not the exception; it is the daily dynamic process that keeps us on our toes and keeps us aligned to the necessary forces of growth and maturation.

Post-Vatican Two Renewal

The transitions I record in this Chapter have been unfolding throughout the past three decades. Many of them are recorded in the US-based research project of Nygren & Ukeritis (1993) and they are vividly depicted by Nadine Foley (1999), recording how one Religious Congregation (The Adrian Dominicans in USA) dealt with the emerging challenges of that period. Beginning with one of the foundational statements of Vatican Two, *Lumen Gentium*, the document states that Religious Life belongs inseparably to the life and holiness of the Church, although not to the hierarchical structure. Religious Life is of divine, rather than ecclesiastical origin.

Perfectae Caritatis seeks to rehabilitate the *sequela Christi* (the following of Christ) as "the ultimate norm of the Religious Life," expressing its following of Christ through the life and mission of the Church.

A two-pronged approach: seeking a more creative fidelity within the life of the church, while simultaneously reclaiming the deeper meaning of Congregational charisms, became the focus of post-Vatican Two renewal for Religious across the Catholic world. New horizons of identity and mission began to open up. This expansion of context is acknowledged and indeed affirmed in the document, *Evangelica Testificatio* (1971) by Pope Paul VI. For the first time, vowed living is described as being prophetic and counter-cultural (13, 16-22, 25). Although *Mutuae Relationes* (1978) sought to provide guidelines for Bishops and Religious Superiors to collaborate on the structure and the organization of the vowed life, the document courageously acknowledges the charismatic nature of Religious Life, and challenges Religious to be creative visionaries in church and world alike.

Of all the post-Vatican Two documents on Religious Life, none is so far-seeing, inspiring and challenging as that of *Religious and Human Promotion* (1978). It launches Religious Life into the heart of the world, inviting a bold, creative presence in building up prophetic communities to activate the liberation of the Kingdom of God. Perhaps it was inevitable that this document would invoke reaction—from within the ecclesiastical domain itself—and this is precisely what happened in 1983 with the publication of *Essential Elements in the Church's Teaching on Religious Life*, a narrow, inward-looking, legalistic statement, obviously intended to curb the charismatic expansiveness which was beginning to characterize the vowed life in many parts of the Catholic world.

From there on, something of the flame and enthusiasm of the Vatican Two renewal began to atrophy. Women Religious particularly became weary of rewriting their Constitutions to pacify Roman authorities. A sense of cynicism and disillusionment began to creep in. Religious all over the world were invited to anticipate and prepare for the Synod of 1994; many wondered what was the point in putting energy into something where at the end of the day the voice of the rank-and-file would not carry much weight anyhow. And for many Religious, the document *Vita Consecrata* (VC) lived up to their depleted expectations. Despite its occasional inspiring statements (e.g., 37, 58, 62, 71ff., 81ff.) it failed to offer a transformative vision for the complexities of contemporary Religious Life undergoing a major paradigm shift in our time.

Renewal Beyond Religion

Paradigm shifts, as indicated in Chapter One, challenge our most fundamental anthropocentric convictions, including many of the ideas expounded specifically in Roman documents of the past twenty years. They indicate in clear relief that something more than human agency is at work, and rapidly it becomes clear that it is not our major institutions that are instigating the movement. Nor is the leading rhetoric, political or theological, throwing much light on the complexities of our time. So where do we look for hope and enlightenment?

Ironically, one of the most inspiring sources in recent decades is that of contemporary physics and cosmology. Just as the forces of creation grow and develop through inherent self-organizing principles (*autopoiesis*), so the rise and demise of major paradigms seems to be governed by a salient intelligence which endows the whole of creation. We humans seem to be in the grasp of a cosmic intuitive Spirit who will not tolerate too much stability and, provocatively, challenges us to consider new possibilities precisely when our projects are thriving—according to our notions of human and spiritual progress.

The crisis unfolding in Catholic Religious Life since the early 1960's did not arise from any transparent laxity or lack of commitment on the part of our members. Religious women and men excelled in holiness, virtue and dedication to God and to the Church. Growth and expansion led us into several new ministries. Internal organization thrived on allegiance. Standing on the threshold of 1960, the future looked bright and promising.

And then, change invaded our comfort-zone, as old securities began to crumble in almost every sphere of our life and mission. And many felt bewildered by what was happening. Instinctively, it began to dawn on us that we had no choice but adapt to the new changes. But it was far from clear why we should change and how we might go about it. Many are still engulfed in that confusing transition, a predicament on which the teaching authority of the Church throws little light or offers little reassurance. Their strategy is to point us to a revised annotation of past principles (as indicated in recent documents). The fiery enthusiasm for the future of God's Reign on earth, which burns deeply in the hearts of many Religious, is largely unrecognized, either by Church leadership or by many Religious themselves.

Risk and Promise

The transitions named in this Chapter are well underway and will not be reversed. Some indicate clear departures from the past; others suggest more modified adaptations. In all cases, they point us to a future that is risky and promising. Indeed, the ability to deal creatively with those transitions is a prerequisite if we are to embrace the new paradigms suggested in Chapter Four. What is emerging at this in-between time is very much more about the future that awaits us than about the past we are asked to outgrow.

The theologian, John F. Haught (2000) suggests that evolution responds primarily to a lure from the future, rather than a blueprint inherited from the past. This observation throws new light on Christian eschatology and on the time-honored notion of the vowed life being an eschatological sign of future hope. In the past we tended to interpret eschatology as having to do with final judgment and reward in a life beyond the present one. Occasionally, it denoted reliance on future hope to sustain us through times of struggle and transience. Today, might it not be the instigation to co-create with our creative God those earthly and human conditions that make faith in the future more tangible and credible?

Beyond an eschatology of escapism, which still inspires Religious Life in other faith traditions, I suggest that we are all called to an *eschatology of engagement*. This may well provide the spiritual leverage with which we can negotiate more creatively those transitions which will require our attention for much of the 21st century.

FIRST TRANSITION:
CATHOLICISM IN A NEW GUISE

Many in the West have not yet come to terms with the idea that the center of Catholicism is shifting now to Asia and the Third World, and that the future world church will not be dominated by Western nations but will be predominantly non-white, a coalition and mixture of many nations and cultures.

ARCHBISHOP REMBERT WEAKLAND

Religious in the Catholic Church have always perceived themselves as an integral dimension of the Church's life. That sense of solidarity became more pronounced after Vatican Two as growing numbers of Religious became involved in the life of the local church, particularly at parochial level. This changed significantly the popular view of the Religious person. People saw us at close range and have got to know us in a much more intimate way. But it raises several questions on how we should be seen both within and outside the life of the Church.

Historically, Religious rarely identify fully with the public institutional face of the church. Already in the 4th century, Religious protested strongly against the Church's gradual appropriation of the Roman lifestyle and values. It is often suggested that this is the reason why Religious opted to live in remote desert places, and on not a few occasions, to refuse even the sacraments of the Church. The tension has been more acute in relation to female Religious. Many of the great foundresses, whose stories have not been honored in Church history, challenged and even denounced the Church to the cost of incurring severe censure, and even excommunication in a few cases.

Since the Council of Trent in the 16th century, Religious have been absorbed into the life of the Church, obliged to follow the norms and expectations set for the priest, seen as the ideal model for all Christian life. Today, Sisters and Brothers are seen as allies of the priest, rather than allies of the people. The essential lay nature of our vocation has been quite seriously compromised, but so has our understanding of the Church itself, particularly its evolution over recent decades which is the material I wish to explore in the present section.

After Vatican Two

In a seminal article written in 1979, the late Karl Rahner, described three paradigm shifts in the Church's own self-understanding (Rahner 1979):

1. The decision of the first Council of Jerusalem in 45 AD to admit Gentiles into the ranks of the emerging Christian community (Acts Chapter 15).

2. The appropriation of Christianity as the main religion of the Roman Empire in the fourth century.

3. The promulgation of *Gaudium et Spes* (The Constitution of the Church in the Modern World) in

1963 in which the Catholic Church effectively declared itself as a Church for the world of the 20th century.

The Church—especially its hierarchical leadership— is often criticized for its rather ambivalent attitude to the vision of *Gaudium et Spes*. As the Church began to engage with culture, there were frequently confused messages on how far Catholics should go in that endeavor. Nor did clergy and lay people move in harmony on every issue. Among Religious, too, there were, and continue to be, some quite sharp divisions: between those radically committed to Christian liberation in several secular contexts and those seeking to reclaim the more "contemplative" aspect of the vowed life.

Meanwhile, a new paradigm began to unfold within Catholicism. In many ways this embodies in very clear relief the revolutionary nature of paradigm shifts. This is a transition now well underway, but neither hierarchy nor laity are aware of its emergence. Subtly and powerfully, a new Catholicism has been taking shape. Its eventual coming to maturity may revolutionize the Catholic Church as nothing else could. It could leave the reforms of Vatican Two looking small and insignificant.

Global Catholicism

This new shift has three dominant features: demographic, people-centered and theological.

Demographic. In 1960, 66% of the Catholic popula-

tion lived in the White, Western world of Europe, USA-
Canada and Australia; that means that 34% lived in
the two-thirds world. Forty years later, in 2000, 75%
lived in the Southern hemisphere with only 25% in the
White Western domain. At first sight, we will attribute
the shift to the population explosion and the significant missionary evangelization of the later half of the
20th century. But is this the real explanation or are
there more subtle factors at work here?

Our interpretation of such a development must include among other factors, a theological discernment.
It will center on the question: Is this a development of
divine initiative, or is it just a secular phenomenon, or
is it something that is happening purely by chance? If
it is of God, then what is God's creative Spirit trying to
activate? I want to run with the idea that this is of
God, and consequently, requires the discerning and
urgent attention of the Catholic faith community.

It means that the emerging Catholic community is
predominantly black and non-Caucasian, poor, struggling and embracing a Christian vision significantly
different from that of White Western imperialism and
that of Rome-focused Catholicism. It also means that
Western Catholicism is in serious decline and has lost
much of its significance as a cultural catalyst. Most
seriously of all, it means that retaining Rome as the
heart-center of the Catholic Church, now and for the
future, grossly dishonors what the Holy Spirit is activating. Continuing to honor and symbolize the Catho-

lic Church as the Roman church is a classic example of seeking the living among the dead.

The vitality of Catholicism today, and the promise of a more creative future, rests with the people of the two-thirds world. This is a paradigm shift nobody set out to create. This is God's doing, following a logic that defies our rational conceptual frameworks and shatters quite seriously the monopoly of Roman, Western-based Catholicism.

Will the leadership of the Catholic Church rise to meet the challenge? Unlikely, in my opinion. The creative naming of this shift belongs essentially to the people. Religious, as a liminal voice of the people, are precisely the ones who need to name this phenomenon with greater transparency and promote it with greater vision and courage. And that leads us to consider another major feature of the new face of modern Catholicism.

People-centered. Priests feature strongly in the popular image of modern Catholicism. Media often conveys the impression that priests form the heart and soul of the Catholic Church. Indeed, a lot of official teaching, while trying to emphasize the role of the laity, ends up reinforcing the central role of the priest.

Today, there are over 1,100,000,000 Catholics in the world. There are approximately 450,000 ordained members; some deacons, most are priests. Proportionately that means that 99.95% of the membership of the Catholic Church consists of lay people, while the ordained clergy comprises 00.05%.

On closer examination these are staggering statistics, and should leave the researcher with some disturbing questions. In a Church so overwhelmingly lay in nature why does a mere handful of priests have such extraordinary power and significance. Why this gross imbalance between the many and the few? Why does Catholic discourse so often tend to end up discussing issues from the perspective of the priest, as if it were predominantly a priest's church?

Several critical issues begin to emerge, ones that Religious in their liminal witness need to embrace and address. The figures alone clearly show that Catholicism is primarily a people's Church. Vatican Two strongly emphasized that the Church is the people of God, in which the overwhelming majority do not belong to the clerical dimension. In justice therefore, the people should be leading the Church and developing its life in a way that would be congruent with the dominant lay reality. But the people have been seriously disempowered, and now urgent remedial action needs to happen.

There is also a serious priestly issue that needs urgent attention. In systemic terms, this numerical imbalance suggests a blatantly dysfunctional system with dire consequences for priests themselves. This small subgroup carries an agenda that has the potential, not just to undermine, but destroy the very meaning of ordained priesthood. Too much energy is focused on the subgroup, and particularly of the type that disempowers the larger majority. Sooner or later, it is sure to rebound negatively on the monopolizing minority. From a systemic point of view, this may be far more corroding for priesthood today than any of the major scandals affecting priesthood in the USA and elsewhere in the Catholic world.

Theological. The Council of Trent reserved the study of theology to priests and clerical students, and that guideline remained firmly in place until the mid-twentieth century. Things began to change in the 1960s. Once again, nobody from within the Church nor from outside, set out to change the clericalized monopoly over the study of theology. Dare we suggest once more, that the change is activated primarily by the Holy Spirit?

From 1970 onwards increasing numbers of lay people began studying theology in seminaries and universities, with even larger numbers reading theology books and studying privately. The first non-clerics began teaching theology (mainly in USA) in the early 1980s. It is now estimated that by the year 2015, 60% of all theologians in the Catholic Church will be lay people and an estimated three-quarters of those will be women.

This, more than any other paradigmatic shift, is what could rock the foundations of Catholicism as we know it today. In this paradigm, the underlying consciousness is shifting significantly. While some of those lay people remain very traditional and conventional, overall they represent a new theological ferment which seeks to engage theologically, not so much with church affairs, as with the big questions facing humanity today. They seek to do theology in the context of globalization, international terrorism, mainstream politics, socio-economics, multi-faith dialogue. The theological horizon is stretching far more rapidly than we imagine. With it the Catholic consciousness is shifting, and since action follows thought, then the outer shape and structure of Catholicism will inevitably change as well.

Implications for Religious

The Catholic Church today is a vastly different organism than it was a mere 40 years ago. Externally, it may seem as if things have not changed much, but internally, in the inner soul that constitutes the living organism, there has been a massive shift. Once we concede (discern) that the active agent of this shift is none other than the Holy Spirit, then serious engagement of an alternative nature is called for. We are witnessing a new face to the Church, one of the most novel and provocative it has known in its 2,000 year history.

Where do we Religious stand with this new movement of the Spirit? This question is particularly acute for Religious working in the two-thirds word. How and where do we invest our creative energy: with the conventional or the emerging paradigm? Are we prepared to put our energy where the new life is, lest we stand accused of seeking the living among the dead? Are we prepared to take new and controversial risks as many of the great foundresses did in the course of history?

Throughout the post-Vatican Two era, Religious worked diligently to forge a closer liaison with local Churches. This often ensued in closer partnerships with clergy rather than with laity. We came to be seen as the loyal servants of the vision and paradigm that belongs to the past and to the euro-centric face of the Church. The Holy Spirit seems to have outgrown that model, and if we Religious are to be truly prophetic, it seems we now are called to outgrow it, too. It is a time for profound and urgent discernment.

SECOND TRANSITION:
SPIRITUALITY VIS-À-VIS RELIGION

Discussing God is not the best use of our energy. If we touch the Holy Spirit, we touch God, not as a concept but as a living reality.

THICH NHAT HANH

Another changing paradigm at this time is that of people's appropriation of faith. Mainstream religion has lost a great deal of its appeal. Institutional baggage distracts from the enlightenment and hope religion promises to its adherents. Instead of being liberated anew, ardent religionists often feel weighed down by regulations and expectations which seem to be more related to the perpetuation of the religion rather than to the spiritual advancement of its practitioners.

Meanwhile, a new amorphous, and often chaotic, spiritual hunger awakens on several fronts. It thrives on questions rather than on answers, on seeking rather than finding, an exploratory journey rather than allegiance to definitive dogmas. Knowing God's empowering friendship (see Jn.15: 15) is deemed to be more real than fidelity to God's power. Spiritual seekers of our time are not much interested in unraveling the big philosophical questions about the nature of the divine. Instead, spiritual seekers are quite happy to risk faith on God's benevolent care and providential guidance.

In some cases the new spiritual hunger relates to a very different understanding of the creation we inhabit. The God of creation—immense, yet very intimate—appeals to spiritual seekers of our time. The God(s) of formal religion—even in a personalized form like that of the Christian Jesus—is perceived as a reductionistic projection of our human need for domination and control. The newly emerging paradigm tends to be quite critical of our anthropocentric projections. Even the notion of a "personal" relationship with God requires us to examine which paradigm of personhood we operate out of (see Gebara 1999, 83ff).

Evolutionary Perspective

One of the features of this new paradigm from religion to spirituality is the attraction of enlarged horizons of meaning. We seek to honor the God who has been at work in creation for billions of years, long before we humans ever came to be. Within our own human emergence, we have archaeological evidence indicating a distinctive spiritual consciousness dating back at least 70,000 years. For much of that time we expressed our faith using elaborate rituals and a range of artistic expressions (as in Ice Age art). Experientially, we knew the power of the divine to be at work in the energy-forces of creation, a powerful Spirit-force animating and sustaining everything in being.

Scholars of religion suggest that we held this divine life-force in awe and trepidation. I suspect the trepidation is more a feature of recent millennia rather than a characteristic of the entire 70,000 years. That the divine related with us in a paradoxical way was well known to our prehistoric ancestors (see O'Murchu 2002), yet it seems that they understood God to be primarily a benign life-force, beyond human comprehension, yet intimately involved in human and earthly affairs.

Our preoccupation with a personal God does not seem to have entered ancient consciousness. God was understood to be a Spirit-power, transcending our humanly-limited notion of personhood, yet embracing all that was dear and sacred to humanity. Monotheistic religions, like Judaism, Christianity and Islam, consider the notion of the personal God to be very central, and go on to claim that this is a more developed understanding of the divine than that held by the other great religions. How much of this concern is about authentic faith in God, or about the need for divine validation for the structures of patriarchal power? That which we perceive to be the primary safeguard of authentic religion—belief in a personal God—might well be a major obstacle to the unfolding spirituality of our time.

Serving the Contemporary Search

Despite several ungodly forces at work in the contemporary world—or maybe, because of them—the hunger for God and for spiritual meaning has certainly not abated. Religious women and men find themselves drawn into this new search. We are often the people in which seekers tend to confide. Some perceive us to be people who can be more tolerant and supportive of bigger and awkward spiritual questions.

That process of engagement with the people's search for a deeper spirituality inevitably awakens a spiritual quest within ourselves. We, too, may find ourselves asking penetrating questions. Our vocational calling takes on new significance, sometimes painfully at variance with how we have lived for many years. And for growing numbers of Religious, disenchantment with the institutional church, and its often inability to comprehend the deeper spiritual questions, can become quite acute for Religious women and men.

One of the more painful issues at this time is that of eucharistic celebrations. Daily mass continues to be a standard spiritual requirement in most Orders and Congregations. For some members today, a weekly, rather than daily, celebration of Eucharist carries more appeal and meaning. For many, too, Eucharist becomes synonymous with the faith journey of a particular local community; sometimes the celebrating priest has no awareness of, and little sensitivity to, that communal context.

For some women Religious, as for growing numbers of lay women, participating in a Eucharist from which they are permanently barred, in terms of the right to lead that celebration, is becoming such a painfully felt injustice that some feel they can no longer participate as a matter of conscience. That very sacrament which seeks to honor the radical inclusiveness of the table-fellowship of Jesus, leaves some women feeling so excluded, that participation seems a form of collusion with something that is felt to be deeply sinful. Western Religious seem to feel this injustice more intensely, but in terms of the paradigm shift we are exploring here, I suspect the unease around Eucharist is likely to intensify rather than abate.

The dilemma arising for some around Eucharist, suggests that we also need to review other prayer structures that belong to the tradition of the vowed life. Praying the Divine Office is an issue of special concern. For apostolic Religious this structure often feels like a ritual being performed out of allegiance to a tradition rather than something that sustains, enlightens or nourishes them for mission. Apart from the prayers of intercession, the themes and sentiments in a particular section of the Divine Office may have little or no relation to what a particular person or group is engaging with at that time. Even much of the language of the psalms, particularly references to kings and God avenging himself against enemies, is patently at variance with the contemporary yearning for peace and justice in our troubled world.

In several parts of the contemporary Church, Religious avail of a wide range of Retreat experiences. This has obviously enriched people's spiritual growth and enhanced their capacity for mission. It is much more difficult to activate something of that same breadth and variety in established communities, where, as a rule of thumb, a type of lowest-common-denominator often prevails, centered on the traditional forms and structures. Unfortunately, prayer tends to become associated with comfort rather than with challenge.

Spirituality and Consecration

A more creative approach to prayerfulness in our communities requires that we give prior attention to the spirituality that informs all our structures, including prayer life. The current spirituality of Religious Life tends to emphasize our special consecration to God within the community of the Church (VC 32, 60; SAFC 8). According to VC (22-24), consecration in the vowed life is based on the anointing of Christ himself by the Father, as a result of which Jesus consecrates himself in total obedience, even to death on the Cross. Instead of consecration for liberation leading to new life (the primary emphasis of Baptism), Religious Life consecration is warranted on rather regressive terms of sacrifice, submission, uncontaminated by the sinful world, holy allegiance to God alone. This is a rather shaky, and unconvincing, spiritual foundation for apostolic Religious Life—either now or for the future. The emphasis is on giving-up rather than on taking-on; it is reactive rather than proactive.

For several Religious today, and more so for the future, the questions and issues that engage us are often bigger than the life of the Church. This provokes us to ask: *consecrated for what?* In broad strokes,

VC (13) responds in quite a challenging way suggesting a tripartite strategy of *Consecration—Communion—Mission.* Our consecration, like that of all the baptized, is a call to communion at the service of mission. And mission, in the authentic Christian sense, is for the whole world and not just for any one Church or formal religion.

Our theological focus is succinct and unambiguous, namely the call of Jesus to all his followers to build up the Kingdom of God on earth. This locates us in the heart of creation where Jesus inaugurates and proclaims this new vision. And the ambience of our engagement requires us to transcend all the dualisms that divide sacred reality from secular engagement. We will return to this topic in Section Five below.

While spiritually and theologically we need to attend to our consecration to God, we can all too easily become preoccupied with it in a way that deviates from our call to mission at the heart of creation. As Religious called to inhabit the liminal spaces where people doubt, question and rediscover meaning, we bring a wisdom and receptivity whereby we must not become over-attached to any one church or religion. We belong primarily to the open-space of the mystic, intoxicated with the mystery of God, embracing the mystery of divine co-creation at every level of life.

In these reflections it is not my intention to set up artificial divisions between religion and spirituality. I do, however, want to honor the living tradition of the vowed life in its skillfulness at reading the signs of the times and responding in creative and courageous ways. In our time, spirituality is outgrowing religion. Many people today engage with deep spiritual questions of search and meaning. Many of those people have never been schooled in one or other religion, and many of those who have been clearly have not been spiritually nourished by the formal belief systems.

This is a new spiritual landscape that the formal churches and religions are reluctant to look at humbly and honestly. It threatens their own survival, more importantly, their own sense of monopoly over spiritual emergence. Religious of our time, if they are to honor the prophetic depth of the past, must not judge or discern this new upsurge solely from an ecclesiastical or religious context. The discernment for our time must acknowledge the Spirit who blows where she wills and has been energizing spiritual meaning throughout the breadth and depth of creation long before religion or churches were ever heard of.

Religious are faced with a difficult and discerning choice between fidelity to the old paradigm with its strong ecclesiastical protection, and the newly unfolding paradigm inviting us to embrace expanded spiritual horizons. I suggest that history indicates all too clearly what our founding people would have done in this situation. Will we have the courage to be faithful to their vision and vitality?

TRANSITION THREE:
FLEE THE WORLD / EMBRACE CREATION

*The distinction between love of God and love of nature
trades on a false alternative.*

MARK I. WALLACE

Of all the spiritual transitions unfolding at this time,
none is more pivotal than our understanding of the
created universe. Embedded in dualistic thinking, the
call to flee and abandon the world dominated Christian faith for several centuries. To this day, the trend
features strongly in the monastic systems of the other
great religions.

For many Christians, the anti-world rhetoric also
evokes disturbing ethical concerns. So much destruction of nature, past and present, seems to have been
justified by the negative way in which we viewed creation. Concern with creation was perceived as a distraction from the things of God. Worse still, the created order was often seen as a place of false allurement, temptation and sin.

Deprived of a more coherent and informed spirituality, we humans often abused and tortured nature for
our own use and benefit. The churches and religions
seemed unable to offer a more enlightened and benign
approach, largely because they lacked an integrated

spiritually-informed understanding of how creation operates. In recent decades this has changed dramatically as a new set of perceptions and convictions began to unfold.

God in Creation

The new paradigm I allude to, unfolding around creation-spirituality, wishes to rehabilitate elements of the vision of St. Thomas Aquinas that have been subverted by mainstream Catholicism. A central tenet of Aquinas' vision was the belief that we could not understand God properly until we firstly had a correct understanding of creation. The conviction is illustrated in statements like:

a) "The whole universe together participates in the divine goodness and represents it better than any single being whatsoever" (Summa Theologica, Q 47, Art. 1).

b) "The order of the universe is the ultimate and noblest perfection in things" (SCG, Bk. 1, Chap. 46).

A retrieval and rehabilitation of a more vibrant and enduring spirituality, for this time and indeed for future times, will need to attend to the following issues with fresh and bold imagination:

1. God has been at work in creation for billions of years, long before humans ever evolved. God's participation in the creative, evolving process suggests that creation itself is God's primary revelation for us. It is primarily in creation, and not in formal

religion, that God discloses divine meaning and purpose.

2. Organic life has flourished on planet earth for some four billion years, long before human life ever evolved. This challenges the widely held anthropocentrism whereby we, humans, envisage ourselves as the supreme life-form on earth itself, and possibly in the whole of creation.

3. As a human species we have inhabited the earth for an estimated 6,000,000 years. We believe God has been fully at work in our unfolding throughout that entire time, yet we often reduce its ultimate and religious meaning to what transpired in recent millennia, particularly in the past 2,000 years.

4. As a human species we have exhibited distinctive spiritual behavior for at least 70,000 years, long before formal religion evolved in its present developed form. But our allegiance to formal religion seems to militate against the possibility of us connecting more meaningfully with our larger spiritual story.

Today, humans are becoming much more aware of the cosmic and planetary aspects of faith and spirituality. This new awareness radically changes our attitude towards "the world." Instead of turning our backs on creation, as some kind of godless realm, there is now a growing awareness that we come to know the will of God primarily through creation and that we encounter God not just in humans but in every sphere of the created realm.

Co-creating with God

For Religious, this is not an easy transition. While some in the West identify more closely with creation-spirituality, in many Christian cultures the material world is still held suspect and spiritual growth is still considered to belong primarily to the inner spiritual realm—in the human only. Integrating spirituality with the exigencies of daily life, particularly in the sphere of justice-making, is emerging as a significant challenge for Religious in the 21st century. This will be a spirituality deeply rooted in God while meaningfully engaging with God's creation. The following are just some of the major implications of this new stance:

1. *Our understanding of God*, not as some patriarchal judgmental figure inhabiting the high heavens, but rather as a wise and holy Spirit who confronts us each day in our earthly abode.

2. *God relates to the whole of creation and not just to humans.* We belong to creation in all its unfolding dimensions. The Spirit-power that turns us towards God is the same Spirit-power that awakens and sustains everything in the cosmos.

3. *The role of the human as a spiritually-informed species.* Our task is not to bring God into a godless domain but rather explore the connections with creation that will draw forth the creativity of God underpinning everything in creation.

4. *The structures through which we relate meaning-fully with God.* Sacred space belongs primarily to the creation itself. Sacred buildings such as temples and churches are meant to remind us of the elegance of God's creation but often have been used to set us over against God's creation.

5. *We need a new sense of ritual to engage afresh with God's world.* Rites of Passage in several ancient and contemporary indigenous cultures are much more adept at honoring the sacred within creation. Christian Sacraments have been construed to gear people away from this world towards a transcendent realm outside and beyond God's creation. Sacraments, as popularly understood, tend to undermine rather than enhance meaningful ritual.

The Pastoral Dilemma

Religious Life has always been at its best when it remains close to God's people, honoring their unfolding struggles and responding to acute needs—unheeded by other sectors of society, including churches and religions. Faced now with a new spiritual landscape, one that often has a deeper resonance with rank-and-file people rather than with conventional religion, how do we, Religious, exercise a responsible sense of mission?

For some people in our ranks, particularly women, fidelity to the Church in its formal context, and fidelity to the surfacing spiritual questions of our time is a combination not easily managed. The Church's expectation is that the primary allegiance of spiritual seekers should be directed towards the well-being of the Church itself or toward formal religion, and to many Religious this seems narrow, utilitarian, and inadequate for those committed to building God's Kingdom on earth. In several cases, we know the seekers will be misunderstood and even hindered in their spiritual journey. Institutional religion, often subconsciously preoccupied with its own survival, does not have the inner freedom to be able to respect the soul-searching of the contemporary seeker.

This is one of the reasons why many Religious in the West adopt ministries where the yearnings of the heart rather than external allegiance can be heard and honored. These include, spiritual direction (usually called spiritual accompaniment), counseling, programs in growth and development, addiction ministry, retreat work, chaplaincy to schools, colleges, workplaces and hospitals. These are pastoral contexts where spirituality, with all its messy and untidy fallout, can be honored, and people's integrity on the journey toward wholeness can be enriched and advanced.

Nor is this an easy transition within Religious Orders and Congregations. In some cases begrudgingly, and in several cases, reluctantly, members have been allowed to take up such ministries which in several cases still tend to be seen as "people doing their own thing." Many of our members, and some leadership teams, still cling to the status, power and public profile of witnessing through corporate ministries in public institutions. While these may render a valuable service to society at large, Orders and Congregations are often unaware of how much their core values have been compromised (as in competitive educational systems), and how many vulnerable people pass through the system without their real needs ever being addressed.

In recent decades, Religious sought to divest themselves of land and excessive property in order to live a simpler lifestyle, more congruent with the poor and marginalized. They sought to dispose of such resources in ways that would benefit poorer sectors of society. What often transpired is that the land was usurped by speculators who exploited it for financial gain. Nowadays, several Religious more enlightened about the sacredness of land and striving to be more ethical in how it is used, are choosing to hold on to the land, while exploring ways on how it can be used to educate the wider public on the responsible and creative use of land. Genesis Farm in upstate New Jersey, USA, an organic farm sponsored by the Dominican Sisters (web page: www.genesisfarm.org), or the Ecological Sanctuary, developed by the Maryknoll Sisters in Baguio, the Philippines (web page: www.maryknoll.org), are outstanding examples of this creation-centered sense of mission.

Discerning apostolic choices today is not an easy task. The problem is often exacerbated by the different spiritualities out of which a specific group is operating. Sometimes fear cripples the potential of the creative Spirit—e.g., I don't talk about how important Yoga is in my prayer life because I am afraid of being labeled as "new age." While fears of this nature prevail, and while they remain unspoken, we stand little hope of doing the serious and urgent discernment which spiritual trends of our time require. Much more damaging is the negative impact this is likely to have on our apostolic options and our general sense of mission for the world of our time.

TRANSITION FOUR:
WOMEN'S REDEMPTIVE RAGE

*For most of the history of the church women have not so
much been denied their being church due to supposed
impurity on the grounds of what they have done, but for
fear of defilement due to what they are.*

NATALIE K. WATSON

Amid the freedoms we enjoy today, for many people
it is difficult to appreciate or understand the oppression to which women have been subjected for the past
few thousand years. Culturally marginated, socially
excluded, religiously demonized, women have been frequently condemned to forms of oppression which at
times reached barbaric levels. Women carry a great deal
of unhealed pain which in our time is crying out for
redress—sometimes in bitterness, occasionally in rage
and frequently for the right to basic justice.

Historians are still trying to figure out when, where
and how the imbalance between men and women entered human culture. Evangelicals, whether from a
religious or political perspective, will argue that this is
how God designed it: males are superior in every
sense—this is divine prerogative! Clearly, this is a patriarchal projection fostering the key masculine values
of domination and control.

Naming the Sources of Domination

Several times in this book, I suggest that one of the key prophetic roles for Religious is to name reality in a way that facilitates Gospel liberation. Nowhere is such a strategy more urgently needed than in the naming of reality that arises from patriarchal domination. Some consider this orientation to be just a few hundred years old (dating it from the rise of classical science in the 17th century), others suggest a few thousand years old (from the philosophical context of classical Greece), and a few scholars share my conviction that the present wave of patriarchy originally arose as the shadow side of the Agricultural Revolution about 10,000 years ago.

One could argue that it reached its zenith in classical Greek times leading Aristotle to propose that men alone are human. Women are complementary biological organisms necessary to fertilize the male seed and produce offspring to continue the perpetuation of patriarchal governance. This view heavily influenced the thinking of St. Paul, St. Augustine, St. Thomas Aquinas and indeed all the major religions—until relatively recent times.

Academic scholars (especially males) will denounce this resume as too generalized and lacking in nuance. This in itself is a ploy whereby we continue the patronage of male privilege, justifying it in the name of rational, logical argument. But growing numbers of women in the contemporary world are weary of the logic and rationality whether imposed by Church, State, or the learned Academy. A new generation of women seeks to throw off the shackles that has bound women (and men) in bondage for several thousand years.

Collectively, women realize that they have been victimized and abused in offering their allegiance to what was effectively an alien and alienating value-system. Also, they have been used as scapegoats by oppressive regimes, e.g., women as a source of temptation for men. Even the very notion of shedding blood to redeem and save is a corruption of female privilege. Women shed blood in a God-given, natural process, as a dimension of giving life. Men usually shed blood in order to take away life. That blood-letting can be redemptive and salvific is primarily a female experience, robbed from the female species to justify male imperialism.

Breakthrough or Co-option?

Although many women, unknown to themselves, collude with the dominant system, nonetheless, there has been, over the past forty years particularly, a growing awareness of what has gone wrong in the past and will need to be rectified for the future. Women have made significant breakthroughs in academics, politics, business and to a lesser degree in science, medicine and religion. But in all these examples, women have been co-opted into systems that clearly uphold dominant masculine values. The real breakthrough—the paradigm shift—has yet to happen, when women and men work collaboratively to create a more benign, inclusive, justice-based set of values for human life and global culture.

For instance, in several Christian churches women have been admitted to priesthood. For some it has been a positive experience, but for others quite a frustrating one. Women went into priesthood in order to bring about change and reform through the inculcation of more feminine values. Their dream had been to transform the system, but in several cases they have ended up maintaining it. This is a timely example—and for some a painful one—of pouring new wine into old wineskins.

The dominant culture will tend to subvert feminine values. In popular parlance, femininity is often confused with effeminacy: a kind of flaccid, passive, emotionally laden, and usually harmless stance. In fact, true femininity can be a fiercely intense and protective energy. Trusting intuition and imagination it will leave no stone unturned to see justice done so that true love can ensue. And where justice has been denied, women will carry the collective rage and desire for wholeness for many years later. Sometimes, this seems to be a subconscious stage of authentic female healing.

Our Western culture, in particular, has yet to learn how to honor authentic femininity. Things have improved in so far as women are being extensively accommodated in every sphere of life. But whether in women or men, true feminine values are still being domesticated and suppressed. Worse still, some women themselves collude with the dominant culture, and that justifies the dominant institutions in continuing to propagate the values of the old paradigm.

Women Religious: The Intriguing Enigma

In Catholic Religious Life women have always out-numbered men and today do so by three to one. Women Religious have been at the fore in every sphere of Religious Life and in many aspects of Christian Life (see McNamara 1996). Yet, history rarely does justice to the women's contribution. Worse still, historians have colluded with the suppression of women and with feminine values in general, occasionally condemning the finest female contributions to total invisibility.

More than anybody else, women Religious should be the loudest voices of protest on behalf of other women—in every sphere of society. Religious women should be the outstanding and outrageous feminists (see Chittister 1995, 11ff). Instead, the female Religious voice is often a muted one, droned out by the shallow rhetoric of clerical verbiage.

As we move into a new paradigm, there are a number of sensitive but crucial issues that women Religious will need to confront:

1. *Institutional Lifestyle.* In several Christian cultures, the "nun" is still perceived to be the heroic woman who has sacrificed all for Christ. Her sisterhood takes priority to her womanhood, and some Sisters them-selves collude with this distortion. Pastorally, they are often perceived as the complement of the priest, while in truth their vocation is of a totally different essence. Their institutional identity often camou-flages the deeper core of their prophetic calling.

2. *Fidelity to Formal Church.* In the eyes of the Church, Sisters tend to be seen as heroic symbols of holiness, with little recognition, it would seem, of how this "heroism" undermines their female uniqueness or, alternatively, as a workforce that does the real work for charity so that priests particularly do not have to get involved in "secular" tasks. Most of the rules and regulations they submit to were drawn up by men, for men, and largely embody masculine rather than feminine values.

3. *Solidarity with Women Who Question.* In several situations, Sisters concur with the anti-feminist values, supporting instead those of the dominant secular and religious culture. Only a minority seems to understand in a sympathetic and enlightened way why women are often alienated from, and disillusioned with, church and formal religion. And only a very small sector would be prepared to unite with women in public protest around basic rights and women's related issues.

4. *Women and Celibacy.* Sexual abuse is often associated with men who tend to project sexual energy outward. Women, on the other hand, conceptualize sexual energy inwardly and gear the creative energy in a more relational direction. Rightly, Sandra Schneiders (2001) highlights the positive values here and what everybody, Religious and others, may have to learn from the counter-witness of this integration. However, Schneiders does not attend to the shadow side of this explanation:

several women in Religious Life frown at the very mention of sexual terminology and become extremely uncomfortable with direct allusions to sexual matters. It is naive to assume that their intimate needs in the vowed life have been met in a more integrated way than those of men.

While the question of homosexual orientation among male celibates has received extensive coverage, little exploration has taken place around what I suspect is a much more widespread phenomenon, same-sex attraction among female Religious. Religious women, still seem to be trapped in the shadow of the demonization of female sexuality which has haunted human civilization for some 3,000 years. When female Religious can embrace this issue in a more transparent and conscious way, we will witness a radiance in these prophetic women which will be shockingly liberating for all of us, women and men alike.

The Righteous Anger

Women Religious are called to be different. They need to cast off the stereotype of the humble, obedient woman, whose loyalty is too easily identified with passive fidelity. While in the past many women buckled under internalized and externalized oppression, today more women are learning how to assert their integrity, mobilize their righteous anger to heal their pain, and become a force for transformation in the world. In this realm, more than any other, is the prophetic future of the vowed woman.

We need to abandon once and for all, the perverse stereotype of the rebellious woman, source of temptation and sin for the perverse archetypal male. The issue at stake is not rebellion but assertiveness; assertiveness for the sake of justice which in the face of past pain and injustice, occasionally evokes righteous anger. And this is one of the feminine gifts our culture so urgently needs. Without it, the task of justice-making lacks nerve, passion and the courage to stand up to the ridicule that working for justice inevitably entails.

The time is long overdue to acknowledge and affirm the central role of women in the vowed life, not just in the Christian tradition but also in the other great faiths.[4] Here we are seeking to outgrow a paradigm that has prevailed for some 8,000 years. Something sanctioned for so long a time will not easily be overthrown, as contemporary feminism painfully realizes. Yet, the retrieval of recent decades has not been in vain and has reclaimed for women (and men) that which has been so brutally suppressed for so long, namely the uniqueness of feminine wisdom. The need to sustain and deepen this recovery—a new feminine paradigm—must become a primary task for all Religious in our time, and for women Religious in a unique way.

TRANSITION FIVE:
THE CHURCH VIS-À-VIS
THE KINGDOM OF GOD

*The dogmatics of recent decades is marked by a steady
erosion of the notion of the Kingdom of God.*
WOLFHART PANNENBERG

Unquestioned allegiance to the Church's laws,
norms and regulations is considered to be a litmus
test of the good Religious. And we assume that this
has been the case since the dawn of Christendom! Even
a meager knowledge of the history of the vowed life will
belie the shortsightedness of this perception.

When Religious Life first evolved in the third and
fourth centuries the growing institutionalization of
Church life was the primary target of its counter-witness. Monks fled to the desert, not just to escape the
corrupting influence of secular culture but also to distance themselves from a Church they considered too
accommodating to secular influences. From earliest
times, Religious did not warm to the power-games of
ecclesiastical dominance. Some refused to participate
in the sacramental life of the Church. And, virgins, far
from being pious women fleeing the world, the flesh
and the devil, were women in protest against the cul-

tural patriarchal norms of having to be somebody's wife or someone's mother. Cultural as well as spiritual factors led to the institutionalized development of virginity in the early Church (see McNamara 1996, 23ff); conveniently, few Church historians record this cultural dimension.

Up to the beginning of the 13th century, Religious women and men were deemed to be lay people. Then began a progressive and corrosive domestication reaching its zenith in the Council of Trent (1545-1563) when the male white celibate cleric became the norm for all forms of Christian life. From there on, Religious were regarded as pseudo-priests and were expected to adopt the norms and procedures of loyal, obedient clerics.

One of the most damaging impacts of the Tridentine influence was the undermining of the female aspect of the vowed life. With the pioneering example of Angela Merici in the 16th century, several Religious foundresses boldly affirmed the counter-cultural witness of Religious Life, especially regarding the church itself. In the words of Joan Chittister (1995, 12):

> Hagiography, folklore and the archives of Religious congregations are full of the stories of strong-minded women who challenged bishops and bested them, confronted popes and chastised them, contested the norms of society and corrected them.

This is a substantial part of the Religious Life story that history rarely honors. For the greater part it has been subverted and suppressed. Only when the full story is told—and women's contribution is duly honored—can we hope to understand and appreciate Religious Life for what it truly is.

At the Service of the Kingdom

Time and again, I return to this alternative view, subverted by patriarchal historiography. Its subversion is also the result of a warped theology, which we glimpse in the age-old tension between allegiance to the Church and fidelity to the vision of the Kingdom of God. The Church has always maintained that it alone can guarantee true service to the Kingdom of God and that despite its limitations; it always remains the primary embodiment on earth of God's New Reign.

This is a theoretical construct that does not stand up well to scriptural and historical scrutiny. While scripture scholars differ on their interpretations of what Jesus meant by the Kingdom of God, there is broad agreement on the following factors:

1. Commitment to the Kingdom was the primary concern of Jesus in his life and ministry, with some 140 allusions in the Gospel texts.

2. Jesus never identifies the Kingdom of God with a particular understanding of Church.

3. The Jesus vision of the Kingdom is about right relationships—in the name of justice and love—at every level of creation. This is a global vision that cannot be reduced to any one religion or ecclesial denomination.

4. Many of the disciples of Jesus, including some and possibly all, of the apostles, failed to grasp the unique nature of this vision.

5. The disciples of Jesus and the early Church began to model Jesus on the criteria of earthly kingship, the very thing Jesus had categorically denounced in proclaiming his new kingly vision.

6. For Jesus, the New Reign of God was an inclusive, multifaceted strategy for the nonviolent liberation of the poor and the oppressed. It is spiritual in its essential nature but not meant to be reduced to any one credal system.

Religious Life and the Kingdom

Religious Life, at its finest prophetic moments, has honored the primacy of the New Reign of God. This often caused tension, and even conflict, with the institutionalized Church, particularly for the female foundresses. Often unknowingly, Religious have honored the bigger vision and placed their gifts and talents at the service of God's people at the heart of the world. Even when Religious agreed to accommodate their service to the needs of the Church, their foundational vision and mission-outreach frequently veered towards larger horizons. Radical commitment to the vision of the Kingdom epitomizes the true call of the vowed life.

Theologians, and indeed some Bishops Conferences, endorse the view that the Church should be primarily committed to the spreading of the Kingdom—see the

fine resume of Bishops statements in Asia from 1975-
2000 (see Quatra 2000; Phan 2002; Kroeger & Phan
2002). Yet, unwittingly, the Church denies that very
possibility by putting itself forth as the only true embodiment of Kingdom-based service. As Religious become more theologically informed, this will become a
more contentious issue for some, while others will seek
more discreet ways to circumvent the recalcitrant
Church. Meanwhile, most Religious are likely to remain largely unaware of this theological dilemma that
carries grave consequences for the identity and mission of Religious in the future.

Religious as Theological Catalysts

As indicated in Section One above, theological wisdom is rapidly outgrowing the narrow parameters of
the clericalized world where the study of theology was
reserved to priests and clerical students. Religious, both
women and men, have made a substantial contribution to demolishing this monopoly. But the challenge
that follows is even more formidable and is likely to
push contemporary Religious Life to the limits of its
prophetic credibility.

As already indicated, theology takes on a different
significance for lay people. Their theological reflection
and analysis tends to be more earth-centered and life-
informed. Their "faith-seeking-understanding" (St.
Anselm and St. Thomas Aquinas) incorporates an understanding of life in its modern complexities of promise and peril. And their deposit of faith is not just the

text of the Bible, but the many texts that arise from the search for meaning in the contemporary world. These include the subtext of several spiritual movements, underpinning the new spirituality I alluded to in Section Two of this Chapter.

For the lay-based theological network, theology is an exciting, hope-filled endeavor, precisely because it is rooted in authentic human and earthly experience. And for the Christian, the scriptural basis has to be one that can speak meaningfully to this context. Here is where the vision of Kingdom enters and quickly becomes the foundation for risky engagement and courageous endeavor. Currently, most theologians, while acknowledging the disparity between Church and Kingdom on several matters, nonetheless try to maintain fidelity to the Church while stretching the theological horizons. This accommodation is likely to become much more tenuous in the years ahead, as theology moves into a more multidisciplinary landscape where the formal Church is unlikely to follow.

The Pastoral Sphere

A more theologically informed Religious Life will also seek out different modes of pastoral insertion and accompaniment. Today's urgent calls, even in the spiritual sphere, are bigger than any one church or religion. The major issues facing humanity and our planet require multidisciplinary modes of address and forms of collaboration that outstretch the simplistic divisions of old. For instance, commitment to justice-making in the future will require skills in, and affiliation to, legal, political and economic expertise. Leaving those skills to "our lay colleagues" is no longer appropriate; it only reinforces in a new guise the binary dualisms we wish to outgrow.

Ongoing formation programs will need to be revamped to meet these new needs. While updating in spirituality, theology or scripture will still remain important, the acquisition of new skills will become much more relevant and urgent. Even though all our members cannot be versatile in the social, economic and political sciences, serious group discernment requires that as many as possible have exposure to new learning in these areas. This kind of intellectual and spiritual solidarity may well become the new corporate face of Religious Life for the future.

From within and without, Religious will encounter the allegation of becoming too secular. Authentic service of the Kingdom of God requires this breakthrough. Religious will wish to remain in communion with the Church, but the real challenge surely is for the Church to become the community it professes to be, one that honors the radical inclusiveness to which Jesus gave his life and death in his unstinting commitment to the Kingdom of God on earth. That, too, is the blueprint that must not be compromised by Religious of the future.

TRANSITION SIX:
CONSECRATION—COMMUNION—MISSION

I hope that reflection will continue and lead to a deeper understanding of the great gift of the consecrated life in its three aspects of consecration, communion, and mission.

POPE JOHN PAUL II, (VC 13)

Although intended to guide and inspire Religious for the 21st century, the document *Vita Consecrata* (VC) really belongs to a paradigm in transition, with a distinctive hankering for the ecclesiastical control of the old paradigm. Nonetheless, there are some openings that can be fruitfully explored to orient the vision towards the future rather than towards the past, one being the opening quote of this section.

The Ecclesiastical Bottleneck

The key concepts of consecration, communion, and mission are open to several theological interpretations. These can be detected in seminal form in *Vita Consecrata*, but eventually get reduced to the context of institutional Catholicism. The more recent Roman document, *Starting Afresh from Christ* (SAFC), indicates a greater openness to the future and a notable stretching of theological horizons:

The call to follow Christ with a special consecration is a gift of the Trinity for God's Chosen People. Recognizing in Baptism the common sacramental origin, consecrated men and women share a common vocation to holiness and to the apostolate with other members of the faithful. By being signs of this universal vocation they manifest the specific mission of consecrated life. (SAFC 8)

Here the emphasis is on what Religious share with the People of God, rather than what sets us apart. There is also a nuanced difference from some of the key statements emanating from the teachings of Vatican Two:

Religious are more intimately consecrated to divine service. This consecration gains in perfection since by virtue of firmer and steadier bonds, it serves as a better symbol of the unbreakable link between Christ and his spouse the Church. (LUMEN GENTIUM 44)

(Religious follow Christ) more freely and imitate him more nearly. Hence, the more ardently they unite themselves to Christ through a self-surrender involving their entire lives, the more vigorous becomes the life of the Church and the more abundantly their apostolate bear fruit. (PERFECTAE CARITATIS 1)

By confining Religious Life to the Church, consecration becomes identified with an elitist form of holiness, despite all the arguments to the contrary; communion runs the risk of becoming a form of subservience to Church institutions; and mission fails to honor the full range of Kingdom-of-God values. Although unintended, loyalty to the Church, (as stated in VC 29-34, 41-42, 46-47) takes priority to allegiance to the mission of the Kingdom.

Consequently, the call to Religious to be courageous and inspiring people, carrying the torch of prophetic illumination, is frequently short-circuited. While this witness often involves stretching ecclesiastical horizons it tends to be interpreted as disloyalty, and then the narrowly-defined spirituality of consecration is invoked to elicit subservience and obedience. Thus the adult Religious, striving to honor adult faith, in partnership with all who search for meaning in our time, is expected to subscribe to a childlike (or even childish) obedience. Little wonder that the Religious Life vocation has lost much of its vitality in our time.

Proactive Consecration

There are several avenues we can traverse to explore the "deeper understanding" requested in VC 13. As indicated in the last section, our primary Christian allegiance is to the Kingdom of God. Just as it was for Jesus, this is also the foundational context for our consecration, communion and mission. Our primary allegiance to God, often explored in VC through rather individualistic bridal imagery (VC 19, 34, 57, 59, 105, 112), arises from our fidelity to the mission of birthing forth new life through liberating communal action. To this end we need a discerning heart and a contemplative eye, two central elements for an integrated spirituality.

VC strongly emphasizes our commitment to Christ and to Christian witness in the world, but it is often an anthropocentric, individualistic Christ, isolated from the relational context of the Kingdom of God. Nor is it a Christ committed to the birthing forth of new life—a primary feature of the divine at work in the long aeons of cosmic and planetary creation. In the context of the Kingdom, spirituality, community and mission are inseparable. We can only have that mind in us which was also in Christ Jesus when we engage with God's world as Jesus did, and relate with love and justice as Jesus invites us to do.

Proactive consecration, therefore, stretches the more conventional notion of consecration towards enlarged and inclusive horizons. These include:

1. Every human being is consecrated by virtue of the fact they belong to God's creation. In the divine co-creativity, everything is potentially sacred, and from the divinely imbued web of life we receive our foundational consecration.

2. Restricting consecration to Christian Baptism is a dangerous form of anthropocentrism, contrary to the inclusiveness which is a central feature of the Kingdom of God.

3. All consecration is for communion and for community building. This orientation initially arises from the Trinitarian essence of the divine on the one hand and the foundational relatedness on which cosmic creation thrives on the other.

Symbiogenesis (growth-through-cooperation) is the blueprint for the flourishing of everything in God's creation.

4. Unstinting commitment to the development of community consciousness—at every sphere of life, including the religious—is the heart and soul of Christian mission, and also the most powerful means to awaken deep spiritual sentiment.

5. While all the religions claim to be committed to community-building in accordance with the divine will-to-life, few succeed in honoring that ideal, mainly because the religions themselves—including Christianity—have uncritically assumed the divisive, imperial ideology of patriarchal governance. This is particularly apparent in the monotheistic religions.

6. The prophetic witness of Religious, therefore, must include a critique of religion itself. Without such criticizing, we cannot hope to engage in the energizing, which helps release the grace and empowerment of the Kingdom of God.

A vibrant theology for the future of Religious Life will largely depend on how well Religious can integrate the tripartite calling for consecration – community – mission. These three dimensions are elements of a seamless web. Indeed, this synthesis has always been the heart and core of the vowed life, as it has been of vibrant Christian witness in every generation. And when faith loses its flavor, as has happened extensively in our time, then revisiting these key elements, and reinterpreting them afresh for our time, may well be the most onerous responsibility facing Religious today and for the future.

This synthesis requires us to examine afresh every aspect of our lives, including values, lifestyle and ministry. The implications will be treated in greater detail in Chapter Four of this book.

TRANSITION SEVEN:
MISSION VIS-À-VIS MINISTRY

It seems that Jesus did a lot of theology at marketplaces.
C. S. SONG

The distinction between mission and ministry has arisen in recent decades, partially in response to the desire to serve the Kingdom of God more authentically. While ministry often locates us in the life of the Church, the call to mission as a Christian people, and as liminal visionaries, often invites us to larger horizons of faith and outreach.

All Christian life is rooted in mission. Everybody is sent to bring new life and hope. One could even suggest that mission is the purpose of God's own existence, poignantly verbalized by the 13th century mystic, Meister Eckhart when he asks: "What does God do all day long?" And he responds: "God lies on a maternity bed giving birth all day long" (quoted in Fox 2000, 41). God is forever birthing forth new possibilities. All God's creatures are empowered and invited to do the same. This is the primary and most enduring feature of the call to Christian mission.

A New Distinction

Mission, therefore, is larger and more encompassing than ministry, and not all forms of ministry are necessarily congruent with the mission of God at the heart of creation. The Church, in the name of ministry, has sometimes supported oppressive regimes, or at least colluded with them. Because the Church sanctioned such undertakings we assumed that they were congruent with mission. Today, we realize that this was not always so.

The call to mission embraces every aspect of creation and seeks to foster and promote the key values of the Kingdom of God: justice, love, compassion and liberation. Forms of ministry which favor the rich over the poor (e.g., selective schools, private hospitals) or uncritically endorsed competitive practices, e.g., the exam system in education, are not congruent with the values of the Kingdom of God. Such undertakings, even when approved and ratified by Church authority, require fresh assessment as we grow into a deeper understanding of our call to Christian mission.

In making these observations and distinctions, I am not trying to create a polarization between mission and ministry. For a long time, both notions were considered as synonymous, and for many Religious Orders and Congregations the two terms tend to be used interchangeably. However, there is a shift in perception and understanding. A new consciousness within Religious Life leads to the conviction that there is a great deal more to our life-witness than just ministry. Every aspect of our lifestyle—prayer, community, personal giftedness, Congregational resources, as well as ministry—contribute to the *raison d'etre* of our existence which is to be people in mission. Mission is a way of being responsive to God in the world and not just a particular ministry or outreach through which we serve God or the Church.

The changing consciousness marks a transition in theological self-understanding, in fact, a deepening sense of vocation. In terms of the emerging theology of the vowed life, we seem to be at the early stages of clarifying and naming this transition. For Religious, it reflects a growing sense that there is more to the vowed life in the following of Christ, than allegiance to a particular church or denomination, articulated through ministerial involvement. The witness required in the name of mission is to the God who co-creates across the entire spectrum of creation, across time and history, forever inviting humans to collaborate in that global and cosmic process of birthing possibilities for new hope.

Mission in this sense is about global priorities, in the light of which Religious feel called to discern and evaluate ministerial choices. And the criteria for such choices are not just the guidelines of one or other denominational church, or faith system, but a true reading of the signs of the times evoking fresh and courageous responses. In the contemporary world, globalization, with the accompanying support of advertising and market economics, dictates indiscriminately the leading values of our age. Globalization pays little attention to either cultural norms or religious values. It objectifies the earth, exploits natural resources, and commodifies human beings. How do Religious of our time provide a counter-cultural challenge to this insidious force? Not without new skills which will incorporate the wisdom of economics, politics, law and the modus operandi of social systems.

Charism in a New Light

In the vocabulary of the vowed life, charism denotes the particular set of gifts a specific Order or Congregation claims to have inherited from its founding person, establishing the uniqueness of its identity amid all the other charisms within the Church, and inspiring the members in their dedication to God and the Church. Charism refers to that indefinable distinctiveness whereby members identify with one particular family rather than another, even though they may be carrying out similar ministries and living very similar lifestyles. Frequently, it translates into specific apostolates, such as education and nursing.

I want to suggest that charism needs to be reconceptualized with a bias towards mission rather than its current link with specific ministries in an exclusively Church context:

1. I want to make the bold claim that Religious Life itself is a charism—to the world, rather than to any one church or religion. In which case, each

Order or Congregation is a particular manifestation of a global charism, the core element of which is liminal witness to crucial values (see Chapter Four). Consequently, in our different Orders and Congregations what unites us is more important than what divides us.

2. To claim that the initial inspiration of a charism is inspired primarily by an individual founding person may undermine the richer meaning of a charism. It is doubtful if several individual founding persons would have launched their Religious families without the close collaboration of other significant people, e.g., Ignatius and the seven companions. It is probably more accurate and historically more responsible to argue in favor of communal founding rather than individual founding. And this invites us to see the purpose and meaning of the charism in quite a different light.

3. Several Religious have tried to respond to the invitation of Vatican Two (*Perfectae Caritatis*, no.2) to return to the spirit of the founding person. But it has been a response of mixed blessings. Some interpreted the challenge as a reenactment now of what the founding person did at one time in the past. Others moved in the direction of greater historical allegiance by recreating historical artifacts of the founding person or of his/her place of birth. What people seem to have missed is the notion that charism is a moving energy of the Spirit. It inhabits living people first and foremost, and if

the charism is not in the living members now, then it has effectively died out.

4. Return to a charism in our time effectively means a communal discernment now of what the living Spirit of God wants to call forth in the members now, encouraged and inspired by the primordial example of their founding person. *It is never a return to the past.* It may be envisaged on what would the founding person/group invite us to do now with the vision and courage that they exhibited in terms of what they did in their time.

5. All charisms are about big vision, although often expressed in specific local projects. In the early history of several Congregations we read stories of a tiny fragile group embracing challenges that seemed to defy all rationality, and often despite heavy odds the group made a distinctive contribution to the world of its time. In this light, it seems to me that all charisms are primarily for the service of the Kingdom, and the communal base from which each springs, itself is evidence to a Kingdom validation and orientation.

A New Heart for Mission

I suggest that we adopt the great foundresses (Angela Merici, Louise de Marillac, Mary Ward, Mary McKillop, Elizabeth Seton, Margaret Ann Cusack) as our primary models for appropriating founding charisms today. These women read the reality of their respective times with disturbing clarity and undaunting courage. They encountered opposition from within and outside mainstream Churches and religions. They assumed challenges considered to be "inappropriate," even deviant by prevailing norms. And they paid a price for their prophetic audacity.

A charismatic voice in a globalized culture must emulate these pioneering women. To confront globalization and call it to accountability in the name of the liberating values of the New Reign of God, Religious today need to embrace pastoral choices largely unknown even in our recent past. Today, our members need to be versatile, not just in theology and scripture; they also need to be skilled in the language and procedures of macro-economics, in the subtle and persuasive powers of mass media, in the intricacies of law, in the dynamics of cultural and social systems, and in the operations of mainstream political systems. These are the areas where the crucible of critical values operates in our time. Without these "secular" engagements, we cannot hope to serve the Kingdom of God in a mature and responsible way.

In the past, "charism" was largely identified with teaching, hospitalization, the dispensation of charity, and care to the poor and marginalized. Today, we are called beyond what was a focus largely on charity, to one that makes justice-making for the sake of the Kingdom our absolute priority. This requires a whole new set of skills for mission and ministry. And the skills for this new endeavor are not so much about individual specialization, but rather about group or communal

resourcefulness. All our members cannot be specialists in law, consumerism, politics, mass media, etc.,
but all our members need to be open to, and supportive of, those who are specialized; all must be willing to
embrace a process of lifelong learning. And where we
are not equipped with the skills from within our own
ranks, then we will happily seek them in our associates, collaborators and partners in mission. Collaboration now takes on a substantially new meaning—far
beyond what it has come to signify in the ecclesial deliberations of the post-Vatican Two Church.

TRANSITION EIGHT:
NEW MODELS OF LEADERSHIP

*Authority functions best when it brings direction and unity
to a group, when it raises the questions that the group
needs to face. Authority does not exist to give orders. It
exists to facilitate the group's ability to facilitate itself.*

JOAN CHITTISTER

In 1989, two American sociologists wrote a book
with a disturbing title, *Permanently Failing Organizations* (Meyer & Zucker 1989). This scholarly work is
actually based on a number of common-sense observations, particularly the notion that organizations over
time tend to accumulate rigid, unwieldy procedures
making the organization increasingly inefficient and
culturally irrelevant. Stalemate leads to stagnation and,
in time, to disintegration. In the face of the breakdown,
leadership often becomes entrenched and inflexible.
They don't understand what is transpiring, and subconsciously, they don't want to know. They cling to the
past, and in the process, they destroy any hope of
embracing a better future.

In both the secular and religious sphere, the concept of collaborative leadership has been extensively
explored. Monolithic, patriarchal structures have been
adjusted into being more democratic and inclusive of

rank-and-file members. Access to crucial information is now so widely available that genuine privacy is difficult to safeguard. Consultative processes have been tried and tested with new models being proposed on an ongoing basis.

Despite several efforts to activate leadership from the ground up and engage everybody in a more collaborative way, resistance to change is still a major hurdle. At a more subtle level, the problem seems to be ideological and not easily named or confronted. Consultation and delegation of power is widely practiced but largely within patriarchal structures where the real power is held at the top. In several cases, change is cosmetic; the externals have been altered but not the underlying consciousness. The core leadership in every sphere—secular and religious—belongs primarily to those who hold ultimate power and rule from on high.

This rigid adherence to power is the primary cause of the abuse of power so prevalent in the contemporary world. Two things seem to be transpiring:

a) The 8,000 year hegemony of patriarchal dominance is manifestly in trouble and disintegrating at several levels of society in general. But those deeply committed to this mode of governance, politically and ecclesiastically, vehemently cling to this model as the only thinkable way of safeguarding law and order.

b) On the other hand, rank-and-file members of society, held in codependent submission for so long, claim power unto themselves with little respect for society's rules or expectations. This is not so much a conscious response as an unconscious reaction arising from an unnamed internal sense of powerlessness. Because this internalized oppression has been kept in place, not just for hundreds, but for thousands of years, the reactionary behavior will, at times, be quite pronounced. It may need several decades to resolve this dilemma in an enlightened and liberating way.

Globalization and Powerlessness

Faced with these trends, mainstream politics becomes more and more entrenched and anachronistic. Political theorists still debate the relative values of Capitalism and Socialism, a rhetoric that gives the impression that these are the only serious political options, when, in fact, they have lost credibility for millions in the contemporary world. Globalization has effectively demolished the nation-state as trade, commerce and financial transactions are now managed and channeled by transnational corporations and not by State governments. The World Trade Organization (WTO) holds far more political clout than most national governments. Even the powerful autocracy of the USA has to submit to WTO regulations.

This is a preeminent example of a paradigm in transition, with many of the key players rigidly resistant to any suggestion of major change. Not surprisingly, therefore, we are encountering a landscape riddled with paradoxes and contradictions. On the international scale, despite all attempts on the part of mainstream governments to conduct business as usual, control is largely in the hands of transnational forces. And they wield power to the advantage of those who can accrue even greater power, namely the wealthy and the powerful. What this means is that most of humanity today is condemned to perpetual powerlessness.

Little wonder then that we witness an accelerating culture of entrepreneurial individualism, with a tendency to elicit solidarity within local, informal networks. It is a survival tactic in a world of cruel corporate oppression. Superficially dismissed as the curse of postmodernism, current scholarship, often operating from Western imperial centers of learning, are largely unable to understand what is going on, or to offer any credible strategy to discern a meaningful way through this confusing maze.

Implications for Religious Life

Since the 16th century particularly, Religious Orders and Congregations have colluded heavily with patriarchal governance. This was the expectation of the official Church and Religious felt bound in conscience and in duty to acquiesce. What then transpired was a progressive trend to accommodate the theological and spiritual *raison d'etre* of the vowed life to the fundamental values of patriarchal governance. Not surprisingly, Canon Law became a primary source of reference for every aspect of our lives. Whatever else Religious did, they were expected to be loyal and faithful in abiding by the rules of the Church. This has seriously undermined the prophetic potential of the vowed life.

It also condemned Religious Life leadership into a patronizing role, whereby leaders often acted like parents, and everybody else was in danger of succumbing to childish subservience. In Religious Life today, we evidence huge reaction to this codependent imposition. Leaders are often bewildered and inept while rank-and-file members fluctuate from infantile-like behavior at one end of the spectrum to total selfishness at the other extreme.

Within Religious Life we often fluctuate between two realities inviting further discernment. There is evidence of a great unease around issues of power, authority and leadership, a subject frequently aired at Chapters and among people in positions of leadership. But for several rank-and-file members this is often a non-issue, frequently criticized and dismissed rather than confronted and reconceptualized.

Those in leadership, and some rank-and-file members, strive to create models that empower and evoke more creative forms of accountability. Noble though this aspiration is, it rarely empowers the leaders themselves. Resistance from members, along with the bureaucracy and maintenance that seem to be endemic to our leadership structures, weighs heavy on those in authority, and sometimes they become disheartened, weary and even cynical. Nor is their task made any easier by Church bureaucracy, sometimes dragging them into protracted legalistic issues.

Little wonder, an opposite extreme tends to surface, and even flourish. It consists of those who seem to be reasonably happy doing what they enjoy doing most, with the approval of leadership, tacit or overt. They steer clear of all the acrimonious tensions that can arise around authority struggles. When the subject arises in discussion or conversation, they tend to remain silent, and when they do contribute it can often be in a cynical or sarcastic vein. Psychologically, we seem to be looking at a phenomenon in which people are striving to protect their individual integrity in the face of disempowerment, real or merely perceived. Theories abound on what has caused them to be this way, ranging from dysfunctional families to postmodernist individualism. We would like to find some way to lay blame at the feet of those who opt out, but perhaps the bitter pill to swallow is the one that suggests that the primary culprit is itself the dysfunctional patriarchal mode of governance that is rapidly losing meaning in the contemporary world.

A Spirituality of Empowerment

Many people within Religious Life will probably take issue with my analysis. Instead they would want Religious Life authority and obedience reviewed in a religious, ecclesial context, one they perceive to be totally different from what goes on in the secular sphere. As a social scientist, it seems to me that the patriarchal mode of governance has infiltrated all social and cultural systems, and there is significant evidence to indicate that the religions have been among the primary propagators of the patriarchal values of domination and control.

If Religious, therefore, wish to be counter-cultural, we need to dream and promote a different model, one that will honor spiritual values like discernment and key Christian values like community-building. Indeed, those two concepts, taken from the bedrock Benedictine tradition of the vowed life—discernment through community—could once more become the animating values for future dynamic leadership, both in the vowed life and outside it.

Deep listening is the secret to good discernment, the ability to see a whole world rather than a partial, reductionistic one. Discernment strives to keep pace with the moving Spirit, whose wisdom and courage always lure us to a different, unexpected future. The pace and intensity of the creative Spirit requires a communal effort in our response. None of us in isolation—leader, or otherwise—can do this on our own.

In our time, it is that cumulative challenge, prayerful and collaborative, that is likely to draw forth the finest gifts of leadership in all Religious. And from that same collective enterprise, we are likely to discover which structures will best facilitate the empowerment for mission so urgently needed at this time.

CHAPTER
4

PARADIGMS COMING TO BIRTH

True vision always is a gift. When it graces us, therefore,
we do not experience "sight" as much as the experience
of "being sighted," being drawn, being enticed into depth.
Our answers then will emerge out of that depth.

BARBARA FIAND

This section of the book is born out of hope. To some it will feel like wild hope and to others a farfetched utopia. It might aptly be described as eschatological hope, and I will venture to suggest that its ultimate but tangible frame of reference is Resurrection hope.

Rational logic will not prove very helpful as the reader tries to make sense out of the material of this Chapter. We are dealing with future imaging, dreaming new possibilities, awakening fresh hope. The average Christian reader will be on the lookout for a few standard guidelines:

    a)   Are these ideas in continuity with the past? Are they congruent with the history and tradition of Religious Life?

b)   Do they support the Church's teaching on Religious Life. If not, how then do we know that these ideas are of God?

Firstly, we look at history and tradition. There is no one history or tradition of Religious Life, in either the Christian Churches or in the other faith traditions. For much of the Christian era, all Religious were basically monastic, and all were considered primarily lay people until the 13th century. Although female Religious have always outnumbered males, the uniqueness of their contribution has not been honored in either the history or theology of the vowed life.

The issue of continuity is subtle and open to many interpretations. There is within the vowed life a deep continuity, the prophetic dimension, or what I will describe in Section Two of this Chapter, as the liminal vocation. This has flourished for several thousands of years long before historical records were known. Echoes of this deep spiritual tradition we detect in ancient seers, shamans and shamanesses, mystics, spiritually enlightened people often dismissed under the judgmental label of paganism.

So, yes, there is continuity, but not of the type that is likely to satisfy the modern reader for whom continuity is a subtle device whereby the reader can retain a sense of control over the story. But the whole point of a paradigm shift is that humans are not in control of the evolving story. We are being carried along by the force of the creative Spirit, often along avenues we would prefer not to go. Just as Resurrection happens "else-where" in terms of the Calvary that preceded it, so every major diminution of a prevailing paradigm alerts us to see the new, not under the rubrics of the former model, but in contexts largely unforeseen and unexpected.

History verifies all too clearly that Religious Orders can die like any living organism, and in fact 70% of groups that have ever existed in the Christian tradition are now extinct (See Endnote 2). Yet Religious Life continues—precisely because of the deep continuity. And that leads to the second set of concerned questions.

Are these ideas congruent with the teaching of the Church? Archetypally, yes, in the sense that the Church feels a need to maintain and nurture those ideals embodied in the vowed lifestyle. Unfortunately, the Church tends to view Religious Life exclusively within an ecclesiastical context, and over the centuries the different theologies of Religious Life often emanated from people who themselves were not Religious. For these reasons the official teaching has frequently lost credibility and today carries little weight, or bears little significance, in the lives of several rank-and-file Religious.

People in leadership—because they are in leadership, and people in formation work, because they do this work—tend to promote the formal teaching because their roles oblige them to do so. But for most other Religious, formal Church teaching neither interests nor inspires them.

As with all formalized teaching, the current theology, as gleaned from documents like *Vita Consecrata,* or *Perfectae Caritatis* (of Vatican Two), offers guidelines largely based on a European ecclesiology, heavily influenced by the teaching of the Council of Trent. Neither document has much to offer the complexities of Religious Life on a global scale, particularly, the engaging questions of the two-thirds world church, where the majority of contemporary Religious live and work. While the prevailing theology cherishes the model of the priestly vocation, it is unlikely to animate or inspire a growing number of Religious for whom lay identity is foundational.

The ideas set forth in this Chapter arise from reflections on the archetypal nature of the vowed life as a cross-cultural phenomenon of great age. Firstly, they reflect the burning questions and concerns articulated by Religious in our time, and by lay people in reference to the vowed life. There is a burning desire for something new, fresh, vital, relevant to our times and not to past generations. Secondly, the ideas that follow seek to honor major paradigmatic shifts that influence contemporary understanding in several different spheres of life. It is these deeper stirrings—culturally, humanly and paradigmatically—that give credibility to the vision I am seeking to explore and articulate.

FIRST BREAKTHROUGH:
THE WORLD IS BIGGER THAN THE CHURCH

Religious are called to be citizens of whatever place they inhabit, children of the cosmos who do not recognize any absolute claims except those of God and hence can transcend the artificial boundaries humans have introduced to divide up land, resources, peoples, and even religion itself.

SANDRA M. SCHNEIDERS

When the Bishops of the Catholic Church convened for the Second Vatican Council in 1962, they had before them several working documents. These were eventually molded into what became the documents of Vatican Two. But the final set of documents contains one elaborate statement about the Church in its relation to the wider world, entitled, *The Constitution of the Church in the Modern World (Gaudium et Spes)*. What is unique about this document is that it came straight from the deliberations of the Council itself, and not from any preparatory subtext.

The promulgation of *Gaudium et Spes* in 1965 was a landmark moment in the entire Council. Several prolonged discussions had taken place with a great deal of divergence on what was meant by "reading the signs of the times" and how it might be done appropriately. A consciousness-shift was happening within the mind of the Catholic Church. It would lead to a massive revolution in the essential nature of the Church itself (see Chapter Three, Section One). But it opened up an expanded horizon for discernment, namely the role of the Church in its relation to the contemporary world.

Enter the New Cosmology

On this front, the Church has fared poorly. The vision of *Gaudium et Spes* has not been honored and, at times, seems almost an embarrassment to Church hierarchy. Meanwhile, the vision has taken root elsewhere: among scientists, cosmologists, scholars of world religions, a handful of Christian theologians, and a diverse range of ordinary rank-and-file human beings.

As scientists probe the big story of cosmic evolution, covering some 12-15 billion years, and mystics of several faith traditions integrate this vision with faith and spirituality, a new interest and curiosity arises on the meaning of creation in its cosmic and planetary dimensions. This field of study and exploration is known today as the *New Cosmology* (See O'Murchu 2004; Ruether 1992; Swimme & Berry 1992; Toolan 2001; Wessels 2000, 2003).

It is new for our time, but in fact, we are dealing with wisdom and insights of great age. And for much of our time as an earthly species we lived and acted out of this big vision. For the past few hundred years, our appropriation of the universe story has been stymied by the emphasis on the mechanistic and materialistic aspects of creation. Classical science tends to portray creation as nothing more than a mechanistic, materialistic process, and sadly, Christian theology during the same period, adopting a strong line on the sinful deficient nature of the created order, unwittingly reinforced the pessimistic scientific view. All of which culminated in the anti-world spirituality that has featured so strongly in our understanding of Religious Life until relatively recent times.

According to the new cosmology, creation is an alive organism in both its cosmic and planetary dimensions. Despite a foundational paradox of creative unfolding and cataclysmic destruction (birth-death-rebirth), creation continues to grow and develop in complexity under the creative urge of the divine Spirit. We, humans, are also begotten of creation, and we come to know God through the revelatory power of God's creation. Our primary role is to be co-creators with the divine lifeforce in the birthing forth of new possibility in every sphere of cosmic and planetary emergence.

For contemporary spiritual seekers, the new cosmology exerts what can best be described as an archetypal allurement. Somewhere deep within the human heart, not alone does it sit comfortably, but it makes sense to a degree that defies rational explanation. It feels like a primordial homecoming to something we have always known, to a place we should never have abandoned.

Why did we abandon it? Sadly, formal religion itself contributed to our alienation from creation. By focusing on the notion of the true God being a sky-God, ruling from on high, and being a God who relates primarily with people—rather than with creation—religion often perpetuated an anthropocentric myth that set up an enduring alienation between humans and their cosmic, Godly context. This is so different from the convivial relationship with creation we had known throughout several previous epochs of our evolution. Our natural embeddedness in the great mystery had been corrupted and we were subdued into an anthropocentric enclave deeply estranged from the grandeur and elegance of our cosmic and planetary identity.

Christians suffer from this estrangement in a particularly disturbing way. The Christian story has been construed within a culture of patriarchal manipulation, congruent with what transpired universally after the rise of agriculture about 10,000 years ago. The Christian Bible begins by depicting an idyllic garden (cosmic creation?), in which humans co-exist largely in harmony with creation. The harmony is broken because the rapacious patriarchal male wants absolute control. To validate that desire, the myth of a fallen, flawed creation is invented and the dominating male sets out on the violent task of trying to rid the world of "original" sin.

This deluded belief, which became a central dogma of Catholicism, and wins varying degrees of approval across all the religions, culminates in our Christian story in the atoning death of Jesus the Christ, reharmonizing that which was damaged, and making salvation possible for all people. In the Christian myth of redemption, people move to center stage and creation is relegated to the wings; creation effectively becomes an object for human use and manipulation.

This is a gross distortion of the Christian story itself. Unambiguously, Jesus opens the story with a radical commitment to the Kingdom of God and the earth-based vision accompanying this dream. In the context of the Kingdom vision (as outlined in Chapter Three, Section Five) salvation comes not through the death of Jesus but through the life of Jesus with the radical engagement in justice-making at the heart of the world.

Today, Christians seek to reclaim that bigger Christian vision with the focus on natality rather than mortality, on creation at large rather than just humanity, on liberation rather than redemptive violence. The new cosmology forces Christians, and indeed adherents of all religions, to revisit their foundational assumptions, and honor God's big picture rather than the reductionistic idolatrous views which prevailed over the past few thousand years.

Religious Life and God's Creation

New horizons invite both our commitment and participation at this time. The anti-world spirituality has grown weary, even to the point of defying credibility. Urgent questions of our age, cosmic and planetary in nature, await our creative witness. Chittister (1995, 11) expresses it well:

> What is needed now is a model of political com-
> passion, universalism, an ecology of life, jus-
> tice and peace if the planet is to survive and
> all its people are to live decent human lives.
> What is yet to be discovered is whether the
> Religious of this time either hold these values
> themselves or will dedicate themselves to mak-
> ing them evident to others.

The following are some of the critical values invoked by the Reign of God as we strive to engage meaning-fully with the unfolding consciousness of our time:

1. *Universalism.* Religious Life globally still suffers from the stultifying restrictions of Western Christian imperialism. Cultic clericalism haunts both our thinking and behavior. Largely unawares, we project an insipid, dualistic religiosity that alienates us both from creation and the wider human population. We need to think globally, interdependently, inclusively. We need to embrace the primacy of God's life and revelation, not just in humans, and less so in Christians alone, but in the whole of cosmic and planetary creation. We cannot hope to serve the unfolding of God's New Reign till we embrace the pressing questions of global justice and multiculturalism in today's world.

2. *Interdependence.* That inflated sense of the human, as the master of creation, is one of the most

pernicious and destructive influences that prevails today. The anthropocentric compulsion to dominate and control, more than any other factor, causes untold pain, suffering and oppression to other lifeforms and reaps havoc on the organicity of the planet itself. As interdependent creatures, owing our origins to the cosmic and planetary web of life, and sustained by it at every moment of our existence, we need to cultivate a very different way of exercising our mutual co-responsibility. For Christian Religious in particular, our credibility now and for the future, depends on how authentically we can address this urgent challenge.

3. *Wholism.* Thanks to the new insights of the physical and social sciences, we understand much better today the interdependent relations through which all lifeforms survive and grow. Nothing in our world makes sense in isolation. Mutual relationality is the dynamic driving force throughout the entire universe. We need to discern and understand, therefore, the systemic and cultural forces that enhance or undermine relationality. Without this awareness we are unlikely to give our full commitment to the new relationships of love and justice envisaged by Jesus in the New Reign of God.

4. *Ecological Health.* Ecology is derived from the root word, *oikos*, meaning "homestead" or "household." As a human species we inhabit several households, and we share them with the other organisms of

creation. A healthy planet is basic to all other forms of health and well-being. Only when we look after our cosmic and planetary home, with the same love and attention with which we look after our personal or family homes, can we hope to walk peacefully and justly upon the earth. For contemporary Religious, our care for the earth, our attention to local bio-regions, our cultivation of land, our regard for food, our recycling of waste, our use of biodegradable materials, our informed choices around the materials we use for daily work, all constitute the moral values through which we exercise our accountability to the New Reign of God.

5. *An Earthly Spirituality.* We are creatures of the clay, carrying living stardust within our bodies, and nourished each day with the photosynthetic giftedness of sunlight, water and air. From our very conception we belong to God because we are begotten from God's creation. From the natality of the earth itself, our birthing God forever brings forth living beings endowed with grace and beauty. Reclaiming our rightful place in creation and acting responsibly as co-creators on the earth is becoming the single most urgent spiritual challenge now facing us. Religious, who fail to take up this challenge, are not likely to offer a prophetic voice either now or for the future.

In the Christian context, allegiance to the Church is likely to remain a central issue in living out the vowed life. And tragically, it is the canonical dimension of that allegiance that is likely to receive primary attention. Meanwhile, the world of our time, and our renewed awareness of the New Reign of God, calls us to enlarged horizons. Many Religious wait and hope that the institutional Church will catch up with the larger vision. I suggest that the responsibility rests more with Religious themselves. As growing numbers become more enlightened, more courageous and less compromising, then our collective voice and our collective truth stands a better chance of being recognized and honored.

This is not a strategy for further adversarial tension, but rather a proactive responsibility for the vocation entrusted to our care and development. In our primary accountability to God and to the work of the Kingdom, we must honor the enlarged horizons to which God has always called Religious women and men. The call continues in our time and we must respond in a manner congruent with the unfolding reality we know today.

SECOND BREAKTHROUGH:
LIMINALITY FOR THE LAY VOCATION

Religious Life must be about seeing what others do not see or saying what others may not say, for whatever reason, at whatever price. Religious must be about the great questions of life.

JOAN CHITTISTER

Throughout human history, anthropologists have noted a universal trend in which humans mission some of their own members into an alternative counter-cultural way of being. Plato clearly had this utopian ideal in mind when he proposed that the guardians who rule and govern "were to be brought into the world in accordance with premeditated principles of eugenics and were not to know who their parents were. They were to live in conditions of complete communism and poverty. . . to spend their whole lives in the service of the *polis* and undergo thirty years of education . . ." (Edwards, 1967, 472). Into the dim and distant past, humans seem to have espoused these ideals, projecting them onto a selective minority group. Farfetched and irrational though the ideal may seem, this phenomenon is likely to endure into the indefinite future.

The process is largely unconscious but can easily be comprehended under the rubric of the Jungian collective unconscious. According to Carl Jung, a collective intelligence permeates the whole of creation. For Jung, this was a spiritual divine lifeforce which we humans appropriate through archetypal yearnings; a creative energy mediated through symbolic behavior, myth and ritual. Through observing and studying the mythic and ritualistic behaviors, we come to know something of the powerful influence of the collective unconscious.

At the beginning of the 20th century, a Dutch anthropologist, Arnold Van Gennep, noted something intriguing in his study of African rites of passage. The neophyte (candidate) was often taken apart from the group for a specific or indefinite period of time. The "act of separation" required a subsequent return to the group usually in the form of a celebratory ritual. The return happened at a consciously explicit level—everybody knew what was going on and consciously participated in the event. But the earlier separation was often shrouded in mystery, and sometimes in secrecy, and this became the unique focus of Van Gennep's research.

Despite the hidden nature of the separation—or perhaps because of it—Van Gennep detected a powerful, subconscious energy at work, one that had a profound impact not just on the individual, but on the whole group. The "act of separation" paradoxically served as a powerfully cohesive experience for the whole group—albeit at a subconscious level. This act of separation Van Gennep called *liminality*, from the Latin word *limen*, which means a "threshold" or a "marginal space."

Several years later, other scholars, notably Edith and Victor Turner, revisited this theory and began to explore its wider implications (more in Alexander 1991). The Turners considered this to be a feature not merely of tribal peoples in Africa, but a phenomenon that occurred throughout the entire human family. The concept includes all those transitional moments in which we step out of the mainstream of life—as in recreation, holidays, worship, retreat time, going on pilgrimage, etc.—so that we become renewed and refreshed for further engagement (see Schwartz-Salant & Stein 1991). But for the Turners the liminality was also culturally institutionalized in one distinctive structure, namely *the vowed life.* Here more than anywhere else, they suggested the liminality assumes social, cultural expression on behalf of the human species.

A New Theology for Religious Life

In previous works (O'Murchu 1991; 1998; 2001), I suggest that this concept provides a solid and creative basis for a vibrant theology of Religious Life, one that seems promising and hope-filled for the future to which we are all called. This is a new paradigm in the making, theologically profound and historically capable of honoring the past, present and future of the vowed life as a cultural-historical phenomenon.

In Religious Life terms, the primary purpose of liminality is what Van Kaam (1968) calls *value-radiation.* On behalf of the human community, we Religious are missioned to be people of value, acting as catalysts on behalf of the people. Recent Church teachings verge on this notion without ever explicitly naming it: "The consecrated life has the prophetic task of recalling and serving the divine plan for humanity" (VC,73; also 71, 80, 105), and to provide the baptized with a more vivid reminder of Gospel values (33). In SAFC, the vowed life is described as "an alternative way of living to that of the world and the dominant culture . . . a spiritual therapy for the evils of our time"(6), "a communion lived in mutual charismatic enrichment"(7).

To appreciate the depth and richness of this concept the reader must forego, indeed transcend, the dualistic conditioning that is still so prevalent in religious cultures. We are dealing with a concept that transcends the distinction between the sacred and the secular, the holy and the profane. The challenge of liminal discernment is to see the potential for holiness (value) in everything, and to unearth the destructive forces that suppress or undermine the universal call to holiness.

The theory assumes that, subconsciously, people always desire deep, authentic values. The origin of this yearning belongs to God who created us all. While at the conscious level we may often behave in a way that contradicts this fact, subconsciously we always yearn for that which is good and wholesome. Religious, therefore, serve as models for the inculturation of key values, not by their own choice but by virtue of the fact that the people have called them forth to do so. This does not mean that we are perfect in our modeling. What makes us authentic is our struggle in trying to get the values right, and explore how they can best be integrated, amid the complexities of unfolding times and cultures.

It is the struggle and engagement that makes us authentic, not the perfect achievement. Liminality is not a modern version of the call to perfection, but the call to grow into that fullness of life that forever stretches the yearnings of the human heart. It has been described not so much as a concept as rather a conceptual archetype (James A. Hall in Schwartz-Salant & Stein 1991, 40) and like all archetypal energies, if not appropriated constructively and creatively, can easily translate into distortions, addictions and fetishes (see Michael Eigen in Schwartz-Salant & Stein 1991, 69).

Identity Revisited

There are several implications to the liminal call that I explore in previous works and will not be repeated here. One point I do wish to emphasize, namely the *lay identity* that ensues from this theoretical base. As Religious, our vocation is evoked and instigated by the people. The Spirit of God at work in the people evokes a variety of gifts in order to further the divine creativity at work in creation. This is largely a subconscious process and its significance thus far seems to have been poorly understood.

Some important consequences follow from this, not least the meaning of the very notion of *vocation*. The sense of calling-forth is very much an endowment of the people. From the beginning of our human story, some 6,000,000 years ago, God's creative Spirit was at work in the human heart, awakening the universal call to holiness. While Christians attribute this call to Baptism, we now realize that the call is far older, wider, based on the fundamental spiritual orientation of all God's creatures, and not just those who are the beneficiaries of one or other denominational faith.

The call to holiness, therefore, is primarily and primordially a people's call. Imbued with an ancient propensity to heed the creative Spirit and a graced capacity to respond, humans, unknowingly, at the subconscious level, forever call forth other vocational possibilities. These include the liminal witness at the threshold places. Our vocation as Religious is born out of the people's propensity for "vocationing."

Because of this embeddedness of our call within the context of the people, our life-call as Religious is essentially a LAY vocation. While the Christian tradition links the Religious Life vocation with that of the priestly state, the liminality points to a much larger and older tradition. The recent teaching of the Catholic Church considers religious to be suspended somewhere between priestly and lay calling, belonging to both but identified with neither (cf. VC, 32, 60). The liminality clearly points to where our identity belongs.

There follows the weighty question of our accountability, which then, cannot be just to one religion or denomination, but to all God's people. Using formal religion as the exclusive context for our call to mission betrays the larger work of the Spirit throughout the course of human spiritual evolution. Inspired by our liminal vision, Religious must strive to honor the greatness of God and God's long involvement in our human spiritual story.

Empowering the People

Today, Religious are challenged to reclaim their own lay identity and by implication to bring into fresh relief the universal call to holiness that belongs to all God's people. This has a number of pastoral and practical implications, frequently noted, but restated here where they primarily belong:

1. The mission of Religious Life belongs not just to the Church but to the world, and the asceticism of the old paradigm, based on dualistic divisions, especially the sacred vs. the secular, is no longer sustainable. The call to liminality transcends all the man-made dualisms.

2. The vocation to Religious Life is a collaborative endeavor, arising from the people, accountable back to them, and engaging their major concerns at all times. In its deepest meaning this vocation is meaningless apart from close affiliation with the entire human community.

3. Various movements over time striving to incorporate lay people into our way of living—formerly through Third Orders, today through Associates—should be seen not as fringe developments, but

touching the very core of Religious Life identity. Currently in the USA, there are over 25,000 associates, 19,000 of whom became affiliated to Orders and Congregations between 1995-2000. Subconsciously, there will always be a desire to link more closely and intimately with people, because in essence that is what our vocation is about.

4. Consequently, at both the human and organizational level, there is a type of gray area, a fuzzy boundary, between the internal reality of the vowed life, its connection with the wider family of humankind, and our allegiance to the whole of God's creation. Church law and the specific Constitutions of Orders and Congregations go to great lengths to establish firm boundaries. This can create a kind of exclusivity which, despite it's practical or legal merits, is certainly not congruent with the liminal horizons of the vowed life.

Liminal witness is untidy by its very nature. What makes it authentic is not the development of neat clear procedures carved out in the prayerful and orderly culture of the monastery or convent, but the messy process, the engaging struggle, to make sense of reality amid the challenges and confusions of daily life. Living out our values is rarely as clear and coherent as conceptual theory states. Ideals are important as they draw forth the best from within us. But there is a theoretical idealism that often cannot be realized amid the ups and downs of daily existence. To push such idealism in those circumstances often breeds a kind of fanaticism that breeds oppression and ideology. The very pursuit of virtue can itself become a vice.

A more responsible inculturation of values is not so much about observing clear-cut laws, but through dialogue and mutual exploration, discerning how best to apply a particular set of values (or laws) in a particular context. Authorities, both secular and religious, are quick to denounce this approach as a capitulation to relativism where effectively anything goes. What they fail to notice is that it is the rigid adherence to unworkable ideals that leads to relativism, often of a reckless nature.

People tend to cherish that which they have been allowed to appropriate for themselves through serious and trustworthy engagement. When people are taken seriously, and treated respectfully, in the midst of their struggle and confusion, then they tend to respond more creatively. Inadvertently, the adult within (and without) is being invoked, and this is what makes the difference. This too, is what faith, based on the vision of God's New Reign, is about. It requires not subservient, childlike persons but mature adults challenged and inspired by an adult faith commitment (more on the topic of the adult in the next Section).

Liminality and the Three Vows

Liminality informs every aspect of Religious Life. It determines in a special way the call to become people who radiate values. This invites us to a fresh interpretation of the vows, seeing them as loci for value-intensification, rather than moralistic guidelines for personal sanctity. In this new context, the vows are not just personal statements of commitment to God and the Church; rather they are assertions of our readiness to work for establishing God's Kingdom throughout the whole of God's creation. All the vows now take on global, as well as a personal significance.

Currently we tend to understand the vows on two levels. They provide a spiritual scaffold through which we channel and express our primary commitment to God. In vowing lifelong allegiance to God, we consecrate our lives so that God can use us more fully for growth in universal holiness and for the spread of the Gospel in the world.

Secondly, the vows embody a set of legal procedures establishing what we can and cannot do within the lifelong commitment to God. Poverty requires us to live simply by following the regulations about goods and possessions as outlined in our respective Constitutions. Celibacy requires us to refrain from all forms of sexual intimacy, on the understanding that such closeness belongs exclusively to the domain of heterosexual marriage. Obedience requires us to subject ourselves to God's will mediated for us through our elected superiors within Religious Life and within the Church.

Within Catholic Religious Life today, while the above is what is formally promulgated by the Church's teaching, among the rank and file of the vowed life, there is a wide spectrum of understanding on what exactly the vows mean. And there is also a good deal of ambiguity and, at times, confusion. More importantly however, is the growing sense among Religious that in the past we over-spiritualized our way of life and that, today, there is a great deal more to our vowed commitment than just legal observances.

That "something more" is the subject on which liminality throws new light. In this context, the vows are not primarily about *laws*, and were never intended to be. They are primarily about *values*. They are expressions of our call to mission—to God and to the people—whereby we engage with the dominant values, and explore how they can best be interpreted to serve the vision of the New Reign of God. In this regard liminal witness faces two distinctive challenges:

a)   It is the role of liminal people to name, affirm and celebrate the values in our world which enhance the growth of God's Kingdom on earth. All that is transpiring within evolution's paradoxical course, and those achievements of our species that bring coherence and fresh hope to the world come under this first challenge.

b)   More dauntingly, it is the task of liminal witness to confront and call to accountability those forces which desecrate and undermine meaning in our world. These are the forces of injustice and oppression, which humans exert upon creation, mainly because of the deluded compulsion to dominate and control everything in the universe.

Against this background, the vows take on a very different meaning, the implications of which will be explored in subsequent Sections of this Chapter.

The Paradigmatic Shift

The biggest challenge in this new paradigmatic view of Religious Life is the expansion of the contextual horizon of the Church to that of the World, as viewed from the perspective of the Kingdom of God. To many this seems a betrayal of what Religious Life is essentially meant to be; to others, it is a futile exercise since the Church will not in any way relent in its desire for total control over the vowed life.

A cursory glance at the history of Religious Life in the Christian Churches makes abundantly clear that the Church rarely has had full control over the vowed life. In early Christian times, Religious Life sought to break away, almost entirely from the Church of the time, which monastic people viewed as over-compromised to the surrounding world. Indeed, for some 800 years, the lay status of Religious women and men, served as a consistent reminder that Religious existed for counter-cultural witness. Not until the 13th century do we evidence a progressive clericalization of male Religious, which after the Council of Trent adversely affected Sisters and Brothers as well. Interestingly, it is from that time on, that the female foundress emerges with daring charismatic audacity.

We are reminded once again that we need to be more

vigilant and discerning on how we read the history of Religious Life. So much of it is construed around the heroic achievements of the male founders, many of whom were priests, committed to the clericalized view of the Church at the time. This is the angle exalted in Church History, marking a sad and disturbing deviation, distracting us from the fact that women Religious have always outnumbered male members, with female foundresses outnumbering male founders. But Church History does not honor that foundational truth.

A bigger story is waiting to be told; one that honors Religious in every religion and culture, all broadly united in a form of prophetic witness, pushing open fresh horizons that help to illuminate the inexhaustible resources of the New Reign of God. This is the liminal dimension, transcending different cultures, religions and churches. This is the big vision to which Religious in our time are called anew. To compromise on this challenge would be a betrayal of the heart and soul of the vowed life. This is what makes us unique and we need to guard and foster it with all our might.

THIRD BREAKTHROUGH:
CALLING FORTH THE ADULT

*As we grow up in faith, we put less accent on individual
salvation and more accent on redeeming the planet. . . .
An adult does not possess a belief but follows on its end-
lessly provocative path. Faith is more like a path than a
platform.*

DAVID RICHO

Western thinking has always been heavily influenced by hierarchical order. Everything in life, including the foundational structure of creation, is perceived
as being designed by God as a top-down sequence—
with the real power reserved to the governing force at
the top. That which generates life, and sustains it, belongs only to the top layers. From the top everything is
given, the task of the others is to receive, and those at
the base are totally passive in that receiving.

The notion of control is the prerogative of those who
govern. Distinctions between begetting and begotten,
active and passive, superior and inferior become significant. And at the human level, those in charge (at
the top) are deemed to be more wise, mature and powerful. Parental metaphors come into vogue, thus rel-
egating most people to a passive, childlike dependency
on one type of authority or another.

The notion of the adult person is seriously compromised. To this day we suffer the legacy of this distortion. The ethics of both Church and State heavily emphasize obedient conformity. Adult self-opinionated
people are deemed to be a threat to smooth governance
and tend to be maligned and subdued. Despite the
widespread use of the language of empowerment, relatively little actual empowerment takes place, because
it tends to be promoted in terms of those who hold
power, rather than at the service of the common good.

The Holarchical Context

Calling forth and empowering the adult takes on
new urgency within several paradigm shifts now taking
place on a universal scale. For far too long people have
been kept in passive subservience. New evolutionary
awakenings alert us to the need to outgrow adolescent
belligerence (Sahtouris 1998) and learn afresh how to
be adult in our time. Some of the religious implications
for Catholic faith are reviewed by Richo (2000, 160ff).
Several factors have instigated this new yearning:

1. Contemporary science, especially physics and biology, highlights a fundamental flaw in our way of
   viewing reality as a linear structure of nested hierarchies. The claim that everything in nature
   thrives on a top-down sustainability has been
   shown to be false. While it may be true on the
   observable level—and that depends on who is looking and how we want to see—it is not true at the
   covert level.

The foundational structure of reality has been shown to be *holarchical* rather than hierarchical. Everything in creation thrives on the principle that the whole is greater than the sum of its constituent parts, and therefore, each isolated phenomenon only makes sense in terms of a greater whole. The sense of belonging, therefore, is not one of dependency on something higher, but one of mutuality within an encompassing reality that is essentially interdependent. The microbiologist, Lynn Margulis (1998) depicts this way of viewing reality as a process of *symbiogenesis* (More on this topic in Jungerman 2000; Lerner 1986).

Anthropologically, this calls forth a radical sense of equality among all humans in which each is asked to contribute, wisely and creatively, for the sake of the whole. This, then, becomes the foundation for the new sense of the adult emerging in our time.

2. At a more mundane level, it is painfully obvious that the socio-economic order in the contemporary world is destructive on several fronts. Because of poverty and marginalization, well over half the population never bring their human potential to anything like full flowering. Because malnutrition, systemic violence and illnesses like HIV-AIDS, millions of lives are cut short. Because of competitive forces in education and in the workplace human gift and talent is often crushed. Because of the oppressive and exploitative forces, imposed

on the majority by the power-seeking minority, authentic adulthood is never attained by millions of people throughout the world; most people never attain the fullness of maturity intended by God.

3. Even in the so-called developed nations, where people enjoy the wherewithal to grow and develop, subtle forces undermine unique human abilities. As already indicated, the major institutions of Church and State encourage passivity and subservience. Research shows that among employed people in the workplace, levels of boredom are exceptionally high, and time off work due to sickness is escalating in many Western nations. Clearly, the workplace does not draw forth nor sustain authentic adulthood, whereby people flourish and find fulfillment.

4. Universally, the education system, with its clear bias towards the capitalistic values of competition and individualistic achievement, is aimed primarily and exclusively at youth. Only an estimated 35% of students in Western nations go forward for third-level training, and in several poorer countries it is less than 5%. This means that the bulk of the adult population is effectively deprived of lifelong learning.

    Pedagogically it is also questionable if our children are really prepared to take their place meaningfully in the world as adults. Schools often set a type of ideological barrier between children and parents. Children learn a whole new specter of concepts and ideas which parents don't understand and often there are no facilities for parents to learn. In most Western nations, adult education programs continue to be undercut financially. At the very time, when more people hunger for wisdom, governments fail to provide needed resources.

Our world has lost a sense of the organic transmission of living traditions. The role of the wiser elder has been abdicated. Indigenous wisdom has become fossilized. What we need now and for the future are educational programs where collaborative modules—parents and children together; adolescents and elders—become normative. In this way, we affirm the adult as a lifelong learner while facilitating for the young a new sense on how to relate to adults.

Principles of Adult Education

Pioneering work on how to educate the adult as adult have been undertaken for several decades. While rarely adopted by formal institutions, methods of adult learning flourish in several parts of the world. In the light of extensive experience, the following principles of adult learning are well established:

1. Adults learn by doing, in a dynamic, interactive and cooperative endeavor, in which educator and learner are equal partners.

2. In adult learning, everybody is endowed with wisdom, the development of which is a joint responsibility for educator and learner.

3. Adults opt for win-win rather than for win/lose outcomes. For adults, cooperation is more important than competition.

4. Adults are people who have attained a mature capacity for relationships, with self, others, the planet, and the universe. Such relationships include a healthy sense of self-sufficiency protecting adults from the abusive behaviors of codependency or excessive domination.

5. Adults don't feel threatened by the success of others, nor do they measure their own performance in terms of other people's achievements.

6. Adults tend not to be incapacitated by perfectionism. They are much more at home with soulful realism. They can live with "good enough" outcomes.

7. Adults relate with transparency from an inner center of integrity, love and truth.

8. Adults are in touch with their feelings and can mobilize their feelings without either wallowing in them or projecting them on to others.

9. Adults empower by giving away their power and this does not leave them feeling weak or diminished.

10. Adults who cultivate soulfulness can tolerate and respect vulnerability, their own and that of others.

11. Adults consider moral values to be important; they will frequently express moral indignation or outrage; their deepest values tend to be spiritually informed.

12. Adults address each other by first name, not be titles; invoking titles as a means of protecting respect, itself infantilizes respect.

13. Adults are quick to express gratitude and appreciation.

James Fowler (1981, 1984) did some pioneering work, integrating principles of adult education into the growth and development of mature faith. This work is well known to adult educators in several countries. It highlights the spiritual capacity with which all humans are endowed, its progressive development through various life-stages, the factors that augment spiritual maturation and those that inhibit an adult appropriation of faith. Among the most revolutionary insights arising from this research is the claim that in most cases adult appropriation of faith takes place in the latter, not in the earlier, half of the life-cycle. This is a timely reminder of the claim of St. Thomas Aquinas that grace builds on nature, and it has several implications for vocation recruitment and for formation programs in the Religious Life.

Vowed People in an Adult World

Two corollaries follow for our living of the vows, firstly, the criteria through which we develop and structure our internal lifestyle, and secondly, the quality of our engagement with people in the Church and in the world.

1. *The internal reality.*

Stories abound about the harsh and infantile systems through which Religious were formed in earlier times. These need to be reviewed in context, one that was often governed by the values of parental supervision with discipline as a primary virtue. Despite the frequent harshness of this approach, many matured into people of grace and caliber who rendered to the Church and society a quality of service that delivered liberation and hope for millions. The disturbing feature is not its prevalence in the past, where in many cases, it was congruent with the prevailing culture, but the fact that it is still adopted, albeit in modified form, in the contemporary world.

Here I allude to the fact that many young people are admitted to Religious Congregations in their late teens or in early adulthood. While undoubtedly, grace can work through any set of human conditions, extensive experience indicates that this is not merely an undesirable arrangement, but one that carries several dangers. This is particularly so when formation programs are run in a school-like fashion, or worse, in a modified military style, with primary emphasis on obeying the system and following the rules. Conformity and the suppression of healthy diversity tend to be cherished values. This is not a climate congenial to adult growth in the service of the New Reign of God.

We are much more likely to honor our liminal call and identity when we invite people of more mature years to embrace the vowed life. Normally, these will be people who have had the experience of living in, and engaging with, the complex world of our time, with its many promises and all too obvious perils. Indeed, the ability to function in such a world, with resilience and integrity, is in itself a healthy preparation for vowed living. Formation personnel can then work with real life experience, discern its wholesome and dysfunctional elements, and thus prepare the neophyte in a much more adult way for the liminal options that s/he will need to embrace at the service of mission.

2. *The adult in mission.*

If our Congregations and communities are to serve humanity in a more proactive liminal way, we need members who can honor the adult in themselves and in one another. Cultures of codependency whether in early formation, or in dysfunctional lifestyles, make liminal witness difficult if not impossible. The call to mission in this new paradigm requires that people engage intensely in discerning the call of God to us in the circumstances of our time. This requires trust, transparency, and open communication. It requires a readiness to risk and explore. And, above all, it requires ongoing commitment to discerning the call of God to a particular group amid the diverse demands of mission today.

Obviously, the demands can easily become overwhelming—always a big risk in liminal engagement. For this reason, the Religious will need a facility to work collaboratively with a range of adult people. This is a different quality of collaboration from that adopted in standard Church practice, where the priest or the sister often holds the "real power." In the liminal engagement, the Religious will often be asked to collaborate with lay people, on their terms rather than on his/her own terms. There is a different quality of mutuality here. It requires greater trust and risk-taking; accountability is holarchical, not hierarchical. A deeper capacity for wisdom and maturity is required.

And the biggest demand of all is for the liminal Religious to honor the authentic yearnings of the people. This requires the delicate task of shifting consciousness to the deeper, unspoken values. But it also means hearing and respecting the deeper yearnings that are arising as people confront daily challenges. When these yearnings disagree with, or challenge, the prevailing economic, political or religious values, then the Religious can often find oneself on something of a knife-edge, a sense of divided allegiance, that requires both the support and discernment of a local community committed to adult discipleship.

From within and without, the call to authentic adulthood is an evocative feature of our age. This challenge is being worked out in a culture still encumbered by so much infantile baggage from the past. Yet, we know this call which invokes the adult is of God, and therefore must not be compromised. Nor can we hope to embrace the praxis of the New Reign of God unless and until we reappropriate the way of the adult. This might well prove to be the single biggest challenge of the new paradigm to which Religious are called today.

FOURTH BREAKTHROUGH:
COMMUNITY FOR DISCERNMENT

*The current discussion of community in Religious Life is
one of the most important and most fraught with anxiety of
all the issues that have emerged from the conciliar renewal
and the consequent dissolution of the total institution.*
SANDRA M. SCHNEIDERS

In former times, community signaled stability and
conformity. Ideally, all the members did the same thing
in the same way and at the same time. Overtly, the
intention was to provide a structure through which
one's duties to God could easily be fulfilled. Covertly, it
was an effective way to exercise order and control.

In the transitional stage of the late 20th century,
community took on a vast range of meanings, comprehensively reviewed by Sandra Schneiders (2001).
Women Religious, particularly in the USA, opted for
single living while various experiments in intentional
living were in evidence in several countries. Among male
Religious, the communal structures often were dictated
by the context of ministry, while many men in the vowed
life hungered for closer fellowship rarely feasible in their
functional living arrangements.

The New Horizon: Discernment

A number of factors have coalesced requiring a shift

to a new sense of what community life could signify for its members.

1. *Nourishing Friendships.* Both psychology and spirituality in our time emphasize the relational dimensions of human and spiritual growth. The emotional distance that prevailed in previous centuries is widely considered to be alien to authentic human and Christian living. On the other hand, the individualism which featured in every sector of life in the closing decades of the 20th century is losing credibility. Intuitively, more and more people acknowledge that we are relational creatures and need relational supports to realize our God-given potentials.

This has led many Religious to explore friendships and human intimacy within and outside formal communal settings. This experiment has had some casualties along the way; people have been hurt and innocent victims abused. Perhaps, it was part of a learning curve in a world where mutual relationships are not easily negotiated. Obviously, we need to learn from the mistakes made, so that cycles of abusive behavior are broken rather than perpetuated.

Positively, there are many examples of close friendships negotiated with admirable integrity and with appropriate transparency regarding local communities, and the Order or Congregation at large. Sadly, these rarely hit headlines. It is often from such friendships that the capacity for mutual discernment grows and develops authentically.

2. *Associations.* Sr. Patricia Wittberg (1991; 1996) has written extensively on the distinction between authentic community which binds people through bonds of faith and friendship, and associations which cover a range of other living arrangements, with a view to serving a particular function or task.

Rather than juxtapose these two notions I choose to endorse Sandra Schneider's notion of organic growth—and often quite chaotic—from the common life, through various associational arrangements towards community living (Schneiders 2001, 308ff.). The common life heavily emphasized structure and conformity. In itself, this led to the breakdown of primary allegiance in terms of mutuality and support. Some people felt so crushed because of the undermining of personal uniqueness that they sought to reclaim their identity by "going it alone." In fact many did not go it alone; they opted for a process of psychotherapy or spiritual accompaniment culminating in a decision to leave Religious Life or reclaim their integrity in a new context. In some cases, this led to a decision to live singly.

There is evidence to suggest that the evolution is going full circle. People living singly have formed various associations, networks and intentional communities for fellowship, prayer and communal discernment. Even people from residential communities at times avail of this alternative experience. Meanwhile those in residential living strive to communicate more openly, and relate more meaningfully, often employing outside resources to animate and facilitate this process.

3. *Leadership and Consultation.* Allegedly, St. Benedict called the monks together for communal discernment around major issues relating to monastic living. Although history rarely recalls it, this process probably happened frequently throughout the history of Religious Life. Today, Religious Life leadership seeks to evoke, foster and mobilize the diverse giftedness of its members. This is felt to be particularly important in aging communities, a dominant feature of the Northern hemisphere today.

After Vatican Two, consultation of members was advocated and, where possible, decisions were reached through group consensus. How to involve all the members and draw on the variety and diversity of gifts, has been a major challenge for leadership in recent decades. The outcome has been one of mixed fortunes. While some members readily acquired the skills for this quality of engagement, others found it burdensome and hankered for the simplicity of former times. Some leaders felt more comfortable and competent to implement this model. Other leaders found the process wearisome, and even exhausting, and upon reverting to former strategies, encountered a good deal of apathy and resistance.

The experience has not revealed a clear trend and the demand by the official Church to retain patriarchal models has compounded problems for those eager to promote more egalitarian forms of leadership. One thing is becoming clear, however: leadership can no longer discern on its own. To confront and engage the complexities of our time, communal discernment is essential.

Orders and Congregations have tried various structures to exercise this discerning process, principally in clusters, regional groups, assemblies and chapters. What is emerging in clear relief is that local community is the primary locale for discernment to happen. If it is not feasible at the local community level, then it will be difficult to mobilize a discerning ethos at larger gatherings, whether in clusters or in chapter meetings.

The Discerning Community

I have briefly outlined three factors suggesting that the local community is the primary focal-point for Congregational discernment: identity via relationship; new patterns of networking among Religious; the shift towards discerning leadership. These, and other factors, invite us to reassess and reclaim the community as the ideal space for sowing the seeds on how to do discernment, so that Religious women and men can become more discerning people in their respective Orders and Congregations.

In the old paradigm, community provided the infrastructure for harmony and organization, so that we could serve God and the Church in a more effective way. Orderliness, perceived to be the primary characteristic of God, was the key virtue in this model. In the closing decades of the 20th century, community—in terms of location and composition—tended to be dictated by the requirements of ministry. Members were assigned to particular communities either by personal choice or by involvement in a particular apostolate. Meanwhile, a new theological *raison d'etre* for community living began to unfold: community exists for the sake of mission, and not just to facilitate ministry. This requires us to explore the meaning and purpose of community life in a much deeper context.

"Community for mission" and "community as the primary locale for discernment" effectively mean the same thing. The community exists in order to discern the call of God in the local and global context, to identify what impedes the growth and spread of God's New Reign, and to discern pastoral and apostolic options to address firstly, what is lacking and, secondly, to explore relevant praxis leading to liberating action. How this is to be achieved in conjunction with Congregational vision, and how it is mediated through Congregational leadership, are issues to be reviewed in each individual Order or Congregation.

For a community to engage meaningfully in this undertaking, the following qualities are necessary:

1. A capacity to relate as mature adults. This requires the wisdom and skills to invoke the adult in each other and challenge one another towards adult growth in the full stature of Christian faith.

2. A climate of trust and challenge based on nurturing mutuality, and a strong sense of mutual co-responsibility for the life of the group at every level.

3. A willingness to grow deeper in faith through prayerful reflection, regular reading, devotion to contemplative stillness and regular review of communal prayer structures.

4. A consistent fidelity to theological study and reflection.

5. An informed awareness of what hinders or fosters cultural growth, locally and globally, facilitating a more informed response on how the community can serve in the capacity of a counter-cultural catalyst. Normally, this will involve engagement with outside resources as well as invoking the giftedness of the different community members.

6. An openness to employing whatever resources are needed to read the signs of the times creatively and comprehensively.

Models of Community

Ideally, this quality of discernment requires a residential context where people, over time, grow into a sense of "one heart and one mind" (Acts 4:32). The group needs to be small enough for people to get to know each other quite intimately and large enough for that quality of challenge and support which this quality of discernment requires. Four to eight people would seem to provide an ideal number.[5]

Other models are also feasible. Some of the best discernment in Religious Life today takes place in *intentional communities* consisting of Religious and lay people, often united around shared ministry. For the best outcomes, the group will need to meet on no less than a weekly basis for a substantial period of time. This will be a time to share stories of faith and stories of struggle, and to discern together how best to respond in individual or communal areas of challenge. This model is particularly advantageous for Religious living singly. Such groups may also include Religious who belong to residential groups, but sometimes look to the intentional experience for a more discerning environment.

The involvement of non-vowed lay people in processes of communal and Congregational discernment has grown significantly in recent times. Not alone does it call forth our mutual giftedness as God's people, it also enriches the sense of vocational calling for all who are involved. And for the Religious woman or man, it invokes with greater clarity the liminal grounding of our vocation as vowed people. Our people continue to call forth in us spiritual and cultural gifts which at times truly surprise us. It seems important that future structures for communal living keep open real options for non-vowed lay people to befriend us—residentially or otherwise—in our discerning mission.

Relating as Vowed People

In the old paradigm, the vows were viewed primarily as laws that kept us on the straight and narrow in our spiritual growth while providing the canonical scaffolding for the norms and guidelines of our daily living.

In the new paradigm the vows relate primarily to how we function in community, internally and in our response to mission. As articulations of the key values that ground our existence—and that of our people—the appropriation of those values requires the committed discernment that belongs to communal living.

To radiate key values in a truly counter-cultural way, and to do so with prophetic nerve and vision, requires both the discernment and support of communal living. This undertaking is too intense for anybody trying to go it alone. The task can easily overwhelm and invoke several self-delusory rationalizations. We need to submit our individual insights to some forum of collective wisdom, and even on a purely human level, we need the mutual affirmation and challenge of the group if we are to be true to our vowed commitment.

The notion of spiritual accompaniment takes on added significance here. We tend to assume that such accompaniment (spiritual direction) is an individual responsibility, with a process and outcome that belongs to the internal forum. The strong individual emphasis seems to have developed around the notion of personal salvation. Obviously it can, and does contribute to growth, both individually and collectively. What is new is the communal responsibility which impinges on how we individually manage our spiritual formation. No matter how personal or private the issues may be, they also need to be reviewed in a communal context so that I become aware of factors that enhance or inhibit my capacity for communal discernment. Acknowledging the fact that Religious, like all Christians, exist primarily for mission, such personal and communal discernment needs to be integrated as a central feature of my commitment to God in a particular Order or Congregation.

How we live out the values embedded in the three vows—which in subsequent chapters I explore in terms of the central values of erotic liberation, right relating and justice making—is a wisdom learned in community, appropriated through communal life and ministry, and evaluated afresh in the ongoing discernment that characterizes wholesome communal life. Rather than being a set of laws given once and forever, the vowed commitment is something members grow into as they follow Christ more fully through the journey of a lifetime. And rather than a goal to be reached at the end of life, the challenge and fruitfulness of such commitment is in the graced blessing to be faithful to the challenges of each new moment.

Fifth Breakthrough:
VOWED COMMITMENT TO
EROTIC LIBERATION

Perhaps, our celibate chastity has never been lived. It
may have been avoided instead. . . . Propriety rather than
passion was our guiding principle.

BARBARA FIAND

The vows are a well-known feature of the Religious
and Monastic Life, yet one of the most poorly understood aspects. For Religious themselves, the vows denote ethical, regulatory procedures often viewed nar-
rowly in terms of what is allowed or prohibited in daily
behavior. For the general public, our vows are perceived
mainly in terms of the sacrifice Religious make in order to be devoted more fully to the things of God.

Commentaries on the vows usually follow the order
of poverty, celibacy and obedience. The new paradigm
requires us to embrace a new language for the vows,
but more importantly to root the vows in creation's own
story, God's first revelation to us. From that larger perspective, I begin with the vow of celibacy for which I
suggest a renaming as the *vow for relatedness*. It is
this vow more than the others that empower us to forge
deep connections that beget fruitful relationships. God's
covenantal relationship was not forged just with the

people of Israel but with the entire spectrum of the created universe.

Life's Creative Energy

As already indicated, the vows, from a liminal perspective, are fundamentally about values, the foundational values on which creation thrives and the call to humans to engage more responsibly on how we appropriate and foster authentic values. Fundamental to all values in creation is that of the divine cosmic generativity which forever births forth the diverse elements of cosmic and planetary life. This is the divinely imbued, creative energy, the divine life-source (God as Mother-Father) who births forth prodigiously, in the erotic power of the Creative Spirit, and embodied uniquely for Christians in the life and ministry of Jesus. Every creature participates in this co-creative endeavor, in what Fiand (1996, 99-100) calls "the transmutation of energy," and, therefore, individually and collectively, we are forever learning how to use this creative energy in a loving, interconnected and responsible way.

This is the heart and soul of what we have traditionally called the vow of celibacy, a narrow sexualized and moralistic interpretation that grossly distorts the deeper meaning of this vow. Sexuality is merely one dimension of the divine eros, a feature of divine gratuity which all the religions treat with a disturbing lack of insight and wisdom. The creative energy of eros has been reduced to a human instinct tainted by original sin, and subsequently demonized as the greatest of all vices.

The Jewish scholar, Philo of Alexandria (30BCE-40CE) translated the central command of Judaism— to love God with all one's mind, heart and strength— not with the word *agape*, but with *eros*. Throughout the Middle Ages, Christian mystics like St. Bernard, and St. Theresa of Avila, along with Muslim Sufi mystics like Ibn al-Farid, Rumi and Ibn'Arb I, often adopted erotic imagery to describe their passion for God, and God's passion for all created beings.

Two writers of the twentieth century frequently cited on this topic are C.S. Lewis (1960) and Anders Nygren (1969). Lewis is known for his description of the four loves, namely, affection, friendship, eros and charity. For Lewis, eros is about "being in love" which in its more mature expression always seeks the good of the other rather than self-absorption, the negative connotation we tend to associate with this word. For Nygren, eros is a form of raw appetite, and totally opposed to agape as love of the divine. For Freud, Jung and the theologian, Paul Tillich, eros is primarily a unitive force.

In more recent times, Audre Lorde (1984), in an oft-cited essay, describes the erotic as the fundamental power of life, "born into us"—and into all creation— through the passionate lifeforce we call Holy Spirit. It is the power for relationship, a passion for connectedness expressed archetypally in the theological notion of God as Trinity and in the scientific icon of the smallest subatomic particles that have been discovered, namely quarks and leptons; these particles manifest only in twos and threes, never in isolation. Creation at every level, whether in the domain of the macro or the micro, in the non-human, human or transpersonal, is primed for relationality. That, more than anything else, becomes the new foundation for what now needs to be called: the vow for relatedness.

In the suggested renaming as the vow for relatedness, I am not merely trying to address the cumulative abuse of human sexuality perpetuated over several centuries, but more importantly the retrieval of the spiritualized erotic energy that begets and nourishes everything in creation. The capacity to relate is a primary expression of what Jonas (1996) calls the "cosmogonic urge." Inherent to creation's evolution at every level, is the desire to connect, to beget new possibilities in a mutually sustaining way. Modern physics and biology illustrate this liberally, and mystics have known it for several millennia. Contrary to the Darwinian view, which sees life as a battle for the survival of the fittest (a view with a strange appeal to monotheistic religion), the deep story of creation reveals a very different process of growth and maturation.

The vow for relatedness, therefore, affirms and celebrates the capacity to relate as a foundational value of God, one that flourishes exuberantly and passionately throughout creation and has been adopted with varying degrees of transparency by all the great religions. Commitment to this vow is a call to witness to authentic relationships at every level of life, and to challenge those systems and forces which undermine life-giving relationships. This includes not just deviant and destructive sexual behavior at a personal or interpersonal level, but all those political, economic, consumerist and oppressive practices which objectify God's creation and encourages humans to become greedy foragers, competing voraciously for the earth's resources.

In living out the vow for relatedness, two dimensions need our vigilance and attention: the *personal* and the *systemic*. In its traditional understanding, the vow focused on the person in isolation, or in one's dealing with other humans. Today, we better understand that human personhood itself is the product of a complex relational web which includes the divine creativity, carbon from stars, photosynthetic nourishment from the sun, the field influences that govern human attraction, bonding, and the capacity to procreate, eventually leading to the birth of each individual person. What each one of us becomes after birth heavily depends on all the formative relationships that constitute one's life experience. I am at all times the sum of my relationships and that is what constitutes and bestows the uniqueness of my identity (More on this topic in Fiand, 2001, 104-161).

Systemic factors continually impinge upon my experience and inescapably contribute to the person I am becoming. All too easily, my life can be controlled by collective forces that undermine rather than enhance my capacity to relate. Particularly significant are socio-economic factors, based on a rhetoric of scarcity (in a world of abundance), dictating many of the key values we are forced to subscribe to each day.

This is where the counter-cultural liminal witness is so crucial. So many people in the contemporary world are driven in a compulsive restless way by forces they are largely unaware of because of the deceptive skill of mass propaganda and the Capitalistic-driven educational systems which do not equip us to judge critically and discern wisely. Lured into the so-called value-free pseudo-culture, many people become the victims of debilitating oppression—precisely in their misguided allegiance to the major institutions of our time.

Our vowed commitment to right relating springs foundationally from our commitment to the New Reign of God. In this original and provocative strategy, Jesus confronted, even with the price of his life, the socio-economic, political and religious forces which were undermining the erotic creativity of God at work in the whole of creation. At all times, that creativity must be mediated through structures capable of honoring the freedom, love and generativity which are central to our capacity for relating rightly. Competitive marketing, cultural indoctrination, addictive advertising, ecological degradation, political power-games, economic *laissez-faire*, the new colonialism of globalization, religious sectarianism, are among the systemic sins that challenge liminal people to mobilize their erotic resources in their commitment to right relationships. Not until these systemic issues are confronted and addressed can we hope to deal with personal and interpersonal relating in a responsible contextual way.

Celibate Sexuality

Having established the priority of right relating arising from the divinely infused power of the erotic throughout the whole of creation, we can revisit the badly maligned subject of human sexuality. We will also need to keep systemic influences in view, because many of the gross distortions that affect our contemporary understanding of human sexuality arose from a very specific systemic context that has rarely been understood or acknowledged.

Several contemporary textbooks on sexuality begin with how the Greeks understood this phenomenon. They then assume that understanding to be normative, and often only allude to sexual pathology as defined by the medicalization of sex in the 19th and 20th centuries.

For the ancient Greeks, males had a distinctive sexual privilege, being the bearers of the seed, through which new life was begotten. The woman, as a passive agent, provided the biological receptacle for the fertilization of the seed and the fetal development of new life. In this understanding, sexuality is a biological process with a distinctive male prerogative. Here sexuality is a biological device at the service of patriarchal governance. St. Paul espoused this understanding as did St. Augustine and, strangely, St. Thomas Aquinas also. We see it reflected in the first formal theology of marriage propounded by the Catholic Church at the Council of Trent: the purpose of Catholic, Christian marriage is the procreation of the species. Inadvertently, what the Council fathers were declaring is that human sexuality is merely a mechanism for biological reproduction.

The Catholic Church changed that teaching in 1962, embracing the notion of a dual purpose to Christian marriage: firstly, the love and intimacy of the couple for each other, and secondly, the procreation of the species. This was a Church very much in touch with a new consciousness in which humans collectively were striving to retrieve and reclaim a long-lost, subverted psycho-sexual story. Weary of the imposition of so much emphasis on biological reductionism, we yearned to relate erotically once more.

The Catholic Church struggled to honor its prophetic wisdom in the 1960s. Since then it seems to have regressed to the more primitive biologically-based view, espoused also by many of the other great religions. Indeed, this is not merely a failure of nerve on the part of the churches and religions. Most governments and social policy makers around the world have not understood the archetypal significance of the so-called sexual revolution of the 1960s. Culturally, we still cling on to the pseudo-biological model leaving millions of people around the world ignorant and confused about the meaning of human sexuality.

A primary function of liminal witness is to offer namings for reality that are transparent and energizing. Nowhere is this more urgently needed than in the realm of human sexuality. Erotic energy today explodes all around us, not because we have become more hedonistic and promiscuous, but because evolution is awakening—more accurately, reawakening—a new wave of erotic liberation. That intense passionate energy, without which creation would have come to naught billions of years ago, today irrupts with an almost overwhelming intensity. What makes it so overwhelming is the repression that has been so prevalent over the past 2,500 years. The institutions of Church and State have little or no sense of what is actually transpiring and, consequently, are incapable of offering wisdom or guidance for this turbulent but unique emergence.

The renaming, which I suggest is a primary task for liminal vowed people, must strive to honor what is deep and original in the story of human sexuality. The following are some of the key foundational elements:

1. Sexuality is a form of passionate creative energy, exploding throughout the vast realm of creation since the beginning of time.

2. Sexuality and its erotic driving-force belongs primarily to the erotic birthing-forth of the divine life-form itself.

3. Sexuality, is first and foremost, a Spirit-infused, psychic energy which awakens in all forms of erotic relating.

4. In the human story, humans have behaved sexually for millions of years and may have gleaned

the powerful spiritual nature of this drive for the first time in the culture of the earth Goddess that thrived throughout Paleolithic times.

5. Like all archetypal forces, sexuality is imbued with light and darkness. This is a paradoxical combination that cannot be resolved by the conventional dualism of good vs. evil.

6. Archetypally, sexuality characterizes all those energetic urges that veer towards creativity; human procreation is one small expression of this creative potential.

7. Human sexuality is operative in all forms of mutual interaction. It is an energy for mutuality, and not just for genital behavior or physical arousal.

8. The marital union of man and woman channels human sexual energy in the direction of the procreation of new life, but sexual mutuality—over several thousand years—has been expressed in a range of other human interactions.

As indicated above, our contemporary culture, particularly over the past 2,500 years, is largely preoccupied with physical and biological sexuality, and seems to be appallingly ignorant of the archetypal foundations of sexuality—divine, earthly, and human. Unfortunately, all the religions display a similar ignorance. Retrieving the deeper spiritualized meaning is essential if we are to break through the confusion and licentiousness that are all too common in today's world and reap havoc on millions of vulnerable people. What we need in order to behave with greater sexual transparency is not more discipline, but more enlightened wisdom. Liminal wisdom and witness were never more sorely needed.

Celibate Lifestyle in Liminal Context

In the contemporary world, some people choose to live singly, either on a temporary or permanent basis. The reasons for this choice, although complex, are conscious to one degree or another. This is very different from the celibate vocation where the choice is not conscious, and if one tries to explain it as a conscious, rational choice, one runs a distinctive risk of trivializing it. As Balducelli (1975) elucidates so clearly, Religious don't choose celibacy, rather celibacy chooses them within the context of a vocational calling that can often feel mysterious and overwhelming; despite the baffling nature of the call, or maybe, precisely because of it, it evokes a compelling positive assent.

Here we touch on the theological meaning of vocation, not just vocation to Religious Life or Priesthood, but, indeed, any calling that requires a quality of response above and beyond the normal call to duty. People who give of themselves with unstinting effort, who are passionately in love with a cause or a dream, at the service of others or of God's creation, are people blessed with a sense of vocation. To the rational, consumerist world of our time, or any time, these people will be perceived as odd, strange or even ridiculous. Intuitively, we know they make a difference, and indeed, that civilization would be seriously deficient without such maverick-like idealists.

Not surprisingly, therefore, we find in all cultures of humanity—right back into antiquity—people who followed a non-marital lifestyle as the price they paid for a radical commitment to a life-calling, which in nearly all cases had an explicit spiritual *raison d'etre*. I advisedly use the word *spiritual* rather than *religious* because the phenomenon under investigation predates formal religion by several thousands of years. We know of shamans and shamanesses in ancient times who were celibate either for part or the whole of their lives. Even contemporary cultures often honor the wise holy sage, as one characterized by an unconventional sexualized disposition requiring a non-marital status, for example, the native American *berdache*, the *kathoey* of Thailand, the *xaniths* of Oman, the *hijras* of India, the *mahus* of Polynesia and the *hsiang ku* of China. In all cases, these are regarded with a certain kind of spiritual respect, commonly attributed to a person endowed with shamanic capabilities.

In the Christian tradition celibacy has come to be associated with priests and the priestly way of life. This leads to the popularized understanding that celibacy is a choice to leave aside—to sacrifice—anything to do with human intimacy and sex in order to be fully dedicated to God. To one degree or another, it is a conscious choice, the fuller implications of which may not be clear until much later in life. Negatively, sexuality is viewed as something suspect that creates a barrier between humans and God. Unfortunately, this under-standing of the celibate calling seems to overshadow all other cultural expressions.

Properly understood, I believe the call to Religious Life celibacy is of a radically different nature. It is a cultural rather than a religious phenomenon with sub-stantial spiritual import for the development and main-tenance of cultural values. It is a disposition called forth in some people by the co-creative Spirit of God working through the universal human community. In this con-text it is never solely an aid to my own spiritual growth (or, the salvation of my soul) but a counter-cultural dis-position through which I serve the people to whom I am sent in mission. In the words of Adrian Van Kaam (1966), it is a core element in the value-radiation that I medi-ate for humanity and human culture.

The non-marital dimension, although not necessary in every case, is appropriate, and in most cases essen-tial, because of the freedom required for the more radi-cal type of service. However, this in no way is a denial of the meaning and beauty of human sexuality, and paradoxically is intended to free the celibate so that s/he can engage more deeply with the psycho-sexual challenges of each culture and time. Humanly and pas-torally, this will always be a sphere of engagement marked by risk and ambiguity, and to handle it with integrity requires enormous spiritual and psychologi-cal resourcefulness on the part of celibate people and communities.

In the conventional understanding, we experience a great deal of avoidance behavior: steer well clear of anything to do with sexuality; as a celibate it is none of your business! This is a moralistic opting-out that has made a mockery of the radical liminal nature of the celibate vocation and may well be a major contributory factor to the sexual priestly scandals that hit headlines throughout the closing decades of the 20th century (More on this topic in Kennedy 2001; Sipe 1991). Within the liminal vocation, we must never compromise the essential divinely-imbued erotic nature of sexuality, and its powerful impact for forging relationship and mutuality at every level of God's creation, humanity included. The liminal person and the Religious community holds on behalf of the human community a sacred paradoxical gift of incredible power and intensity. Our vocation is to facilitate a responsible and creative exploration and appropriation of this gift within the changing contexts of different times and cultures. No task could be more onerous and noble; nor could there be one that is so awesome and potentially bewildering in what it asks of us.

In liminal witness, therefore, we must question and contest, the excessive biologization of human sexuality that has prevailed over the past 2,500 years. It is a cultural aberration that has long outlived its usefulness, leading to most if not all the outrageous abuse of sexuality that prevails in the contemporary world. It is not a case of us setting ourselves up in opposition to church or religion. It is liminal witness doing what it is meant to do: stretching the horizons of meaning to greater depth and authenticity. Anything short of this is a betrayal of what God—and God's people—are calling us to be.

How do the Sexual Liminars Care for Themselves?

In the current climate of sexual abuse by priests and Religious, the main interest is not so much in a better understanding of the celibate vocation—as I attempt to offer here—but rather in how celibates can be helped to manage their own sexual behavior in more congruent and responsible ways. Present expectations are sadly shortsighted, very much focused on symptoms rather than on contributing causes. Two Reports issued in 2004 on the abuse of minors by priests in USA, laid the blame firmly at the door of admission standards, suggesting that the deviant behaviors of later years were already lurking within those people when they entered Seminary. A very convenient way of avoiding a range of more serious questions, and in many cases, I suggest a verdict that is grossly inaccurate!

What makes responsible sexual living difficult for celibates is precisely the same range of factors that makes it difficult for people in general. Foremost in this range is the grossly distorted view of human sexuality we have appropriated for over 2,000 years. While we continue to biologize sexuality we will keep turning it into a pathological monstrosity. While we continue to retain primary emphasis on sex for procreation we inevitably invite a cult of sex for recreation. The reductionism in one sphere creates a more aberrant reductionism in another sphere. We need to break this cycle, not just of abusive behavior, but of abusive, distorted perceptions. It is the understanding of sexuality that is aberrant, immoral and pathological, and if the consciousness is defective, inevitably so will be the action.

For the Religious Life person, therefore, the following are some of the inherently "protective" measures that make celibate living more creative, generative and responsible:

1. A holistic understanding of what sexuality is about, coupled with a life-experience in which one has had time and opportunity to explore how one has inculturated sexual values, personally and culturally. An obvious corollary follows here: celibate liminal living is really for adults who have had adequate time to experience life in ordinary daily living at the heart of the world.

2. A reasonable degree of comfort with the amorphous and indefinable nature of one's sexual identity. Many celibates, and several shaman-like figures in the past, manifest strong androgynous characteristics. Perhaps, this is what makes the celibate genuinely liminal: his/her sexuality embraces not merely a strong masculine-feminine duality but also an ongoing male-female process of integration which is precisely what empowers the celibate to be a cultural catalyst for people of all sexual orientations and struggles.

3. A mature adult spirituality focused on the adult
    God of unconditional love, a God who invites and
    empowers every liminal celibate for passionate en-
    gagement with all who search for authentic love
    and intimacy in their lives.

4. Regular spiritual and psychological resources for re-
    view and support as one engages with weighty and
    intense emotional issues that belong to sexual living.

5. A supportive community—residential or inten-
    tional—a context where one can be at home both
    with the deep inexplicable satisfaction of one's call-
    ing while also knowing that there are soulmates
    who can understand and support when the passion
    of engagement comes close to breaking-point.

6. A circle of close friends with which one can enjoy
    nourishing exchanges of tenderness and care.

And with all that taken on board, we know we are
dealing with something verging on the impossible. Were
it not for the grace of God, and the power of God's unconditional, erotic love, none of us could ever hope to
dream such dreams or entertain such aspirations. Our
God has always called forth liminal celibates and no
doubt will in the future. And when the dust settles on
all the shortsighted analysis of contemporary scandals,
and the millions who have been sexually abused begin
to come home to their erotic selves, then we have every
reason to hope that celibate sexuality will once more
become the gem in the crown that it has been in the
vowed life for much longer than any of us realize.

SIXTH BREAKTHROUGH:
VOWED COMMITMENT TO JUSTICE-MAKING

Too often, the church has understood God's unconditional grace as solely a theological phenomenon, instead of recognizing that it has to do with the reordering of the economy of the world.

WALTER BRUEGGEMANN

God's call to humanity to co-create towards a world of right relationships is the basis on which I propose a radical redesign of the three vows upon which Religious pronounce their commitment to God and to God's world. The focus on right relating is primordially expressed in the Vow for Relatedness. The other two vows, traditionally referred to as *poverty* and *obedience*, invite us to look at the strategies and structures that enhance or hinder the divinely desired relational matrix—poverty, attending more to strategies, and obedience, to structures.

We once again note the incongruence and irrelevance of traditional language. Poverty is an evil that Jesus did everything in his power to get rid of; so must those who seek to follow Jesus in a serious way. I have suggested elsewhere that we rename the vow of poverty as a *vow for mutual sustainability*, perhaps more accurately a *vow for justice-making.* And the word *obe-dience* carries several oppressive patriarchal overtones; I suggest a renaming as the vow *for mutual collabora-tion* in which we explore the structures best suited to build a culture of right relating in accordance with God's will for humanity, for the planet and the cosmos.

Life as Gift

The vow for mutual sustainability (poverty) begins with the acknowledgement that from God's perspective everything in creation is given as pure gift. From the vast galaxies to the unique capacity of each microbe, *gifted-ness* is the foundational quality of everything in creation. And the giftedness is not just for the sake of humans, but for the elegance of creation itself. As creatures of God's creation our first privilege and duty is to contemplate the elegance and beauty of the creation we inhabit and the earth to which we intimately belong.

While all three vows begin from a contemplative gaze, it is particularly so in the case of the vow for mutual sustainability. Whereas the vow for relatedness names the erotic power of God's energy in creation, the vow for mutual sustainability names and invites us to celebrate God's boundless giftedness. And in a world constructed on the basis of such giftedness, all creatures and especially us, humans, need to learn how to engage convivially with the creation that sur-rounds us. Utopian though this ideal may be, such is the liminal challenge that faces all people committed to the vowed life.

There is a related feature which becomes even more haunting for the human race, namely, the fact that God's generous giving is without condition. Unconditional love, noted in our exposition of the last vow, is the basis of the prodigious giftedness. We are the beneficiaries of a creation resplendently endowed. There is more than enough for everybody to enjoy life richly. We know of course, that this is not how the majority of human beings experience life! Not because of some fundamental flaw in creation, but because humanity today is stuck in its allegiance to the marauding plunder of patriarchal dominance, and, consequently, seems unable and unwilling to befriend the foundational giftedness of everything we have been given in God's prodigious creation.

Those committed to the vowed life must not compromise the liminal and prophetic task of naming reality from God's perspective. Idealistic though it may seem the essential nature of our vocation is to honor the divine prerogative across the entire splendor of God's birthing forth, as revealed in the whole cosmos. Creation is not merely a material resource for mankind's use and benefit. Creation is the landscape and context of God's original revelation to us, the primary mirror in which we see the face of God and conceptualize how God wants us to live and behave as creatures of planet earth.

In the liminal context, all the vows take on global and cosmic meaning. Yet, the practical implications in all three cases are very specific and grounded in the daily grind of ordinary life. To reflective people of our planet today, it must surely be obvious that all is not right between us and creation, that something quite serious is out of kilter, and that the ultimate consequences for humanity look more precarious with each passing day. Nor do those same reflective people give much credibility to the theory of a flawed creation. Increasingly, it is becoming obvious that creation is not the problem; human beings are!

Naming the Pain of Creation

The liminal naming of our contorted relationship with creation needs to begin with what Brueggemann (1986) calls the prophetic lament. As a species we need to learn how to grieve and lament for the pain of creation—the very pain we try so desperately to keep at bay by hedonistic pleasure, addictive behaviors and the romanticization of violence. We keep running away from our own destructiveness, and we will keep doing so unless and until prophetic liminal people call us to our senses.

We have raped the womb of our planetary groundedness. We have objectified the divine energy that flows through the veins of creation in its air and water systems. We randomly exploit and abuse on a massive scale. And then in what must be one of the greatest blasphemies of humanity, spiritual writers attribute our alienation to a faulty relationship with God. God is not the source or cause of our alienation or estrangement; our wrong relationship with God's creation is what has cast us into exile.

Our prophetic lament and cultural grief is a pre-condition for a conversion process that embraces a number of stages:

a) The humble admission that we humans have not got it right with creation; even the religions have it basically wrong, and this is not God's fault but our own.

b) The willingness to lament for what we have done. This will help relieve the inner hurt (alienation) we all carry because we have become disconnected from our primordial womb.

c) The readiness to invoke the prophetic imagination to embrace alternative ways of engaging with creation, more congruent with God's creative birthing-forth.

d) The trust to let new wisdom surface from the margins to which most people have been consigned against their will, and listen to their dreams for an alternative way of being.

e) Activating a collaborative spirit to work towards "a new heaven and a new earth" where the values of the Kingdom of God become more transparent and proactive.

f) The education and formation in justice-making, to rectify the wrongs that marginalize the earth, its resources and most of its people.

This ideal vision, and its accompanying aspirations, are incumbent upon liminal people, not just because of a Gospel mandate but because the very future of humanity itself requires us to act in this way. There is abundant research to show that the human race cannot—and will not—continue on its present course, because the limited resources of creation will not allow it. Creation's ecosystems can only continue to thrive within relational parameters that are quite specific and require humanity to behave with a greater sense of gentleness, frugality and respect. The Darwinian notion of the earth adapting to new pressures, and thus continuing to thrive in spite of humanity's voracious use of resources, is no longer credible. Evolutionary adaptations tend to be slow and gradual; the current devastation of natural resources is pushing ecological sustainability beyond the limits innate to nature's growth and flourishing.

Perhaps, the greatest resistance to the prophetic lament rests in the naïve assumption that even if we humans destroy the earth, we ourselves will somehow survive. Without a meaningful earth, our own lives become quite meaningless; without an organically healthy planet, our own health becomes seriously depleted, and then we end up creating medicalized healthcare to rectify the dysfunctional illnesses we drew upon ourselves. Our call to repentance and to prophetic lament is precisely a call to see more clearly the convoluted quagmire in which we have engulfed ourselves. Paradoxically, it is our willingness to grieve that will empower us to break loose from that quagmire and begin to reclaim the freedom our God wishes us to live by.

The Sin of Dislocation

Prevallet (2000, 23) suggests that we revision the vow for mutual sustainability in terms of the root *chakra* in the human energy field. This is the energy constellation (at the base of the spine) that grounds our humanity, keeps us close to the earth, and attuned to all our God bestows through the earth for our human flourishing. In today's world many people are not appropriately grounded in creation. Firstly, our formative years, in family and homestead, often lack an authentic sense of space. In our time, we know extensive human mobility, sometimes of an enforced nature, as for refugees. And for the growing numbers who inhabit urban sprawls, place does not have the same bio-regional or visceral sense of connection that one experiences in a rural setting.

Secondly, the produce of creation we consume each day has largely lost the sense of local connection. Because of mass production and current global trade, increasing numbers of people have no idea where their food comes from, nor do they understand much about the growth and production of food. In the Christian Eucharist we pray the words: "fruit of the earth and the work of human hands," but for many people these words do not correspond to lived experience. In the West generally, and in urban settings around the world, people rarely evidence fruit being sown or reaped, nor do their "hands" engage with that process. Little wonder we feel so estranged from the womb of our origins.

Land has lost a great deal of the sacredness it holds in all the religious traditions—and these are only poor reflections of the sacred regard in which earth was honored in prehistoric times. In the contemporary consciousness, land like so much else in creation, is an object, a commodity, used and exploited to make money. This aberration began with the fracturing of the planet in post-Agricultural times, beginning about 5,000 years ago, and culminated in the creation of nation states, initially in Greek and Roman times and in the African subcontinent in the mid-twentieth century. Today the ideology of the nation-state is coming full circle with transnational corporations rapidly robbing several states of their political and economic status.

This is creating a dangerous and largely unrecognized vacuum, urgently awaiting liminal naming. So many religions regard the nation-state to be of divine origin, an expression of God's will for planet earth. Many bitter and destructive wars have been fought over nation-states. The nation-state is a planetary expression of the patriarchal compulsion to divide-and-conquer. It is not of God, but of man—quite literally. And with the progressive breakdown of that institution, we evidence huge social and political dislocation in the modern world. In theory, the nation-state is still "in control" but it is becoming daily apparent that all the major issues facing humanity—terrorism, trade, environmental responsibility, use of natural resources, etc. require transnational agencies to facilitate international transactions. We face a new planetary and human crisis for which we are ill-prepared.

Many readers will wonder why these weighty, economic and political issues arise in a book on Religious Life. The call to liminal and prophetic witness requires us to visit every issue that affects the values out of which we live. Most of the values in today's world are dictated, not by churches and religions, and not even by national governments, but by transnational forces in the face of which we feel a growing sense of powerlessness. Our God never intended us to be powerless and paralyzed in the face of such challenges. In the face of these momentous challenges, mainstream institutions, religious and secular, can do little, if indeed anything, to empower us. We need a radically new vision, and those committed to the values of mutual sustainability occupy the liminal space from which the new vision can be articulated and brought to birth.

Justice-making

The new vision I refer to has justice-making as a core, central element. Although all the churches and religions adopt this as a key value, it is given a great deal of rhetoric, but not much practical expression. Institutions operating out a patriarchal will-to-power are not capable of being just. Power tends to be self-perpetuating and in time erodes the will to justice. Power only knows one mode of relating with the binary poles of domination and subservience. Justice, or what St. Paul describes as *righteousness*, is about a process of relating in what Fiorenza (1993) calls a discipleship of equals. Structurally, justice is egalitarian rather than patriarchal, holarchical rather than hierarchical. And the modus operandi is also very different. Power is essentially linear with the supreme authority at the top; justice-making is lateral, and much more at home in a networking approach.

Many people equate justice-making with local "peace and justice" groups. Others will identify it with what the rich West should do for the poor South. In either case, what is being named is a state of affairs in which the goods of creation are not fairly distributed to everybody's advantage. And the motivation behind such work, is the conviction, variously expressed, that God wants everybody treated equally and fairly. Therefore the vow for mutual sustainability, like the other vows, begins with the desire to align our wills with God's will. Clearly, the affairs of our world are not governed in a Godlike way despite all the rhetoric to the contrary. And it is becoming all too clear, that governance of the future is leading towards Godlessness, not to Godlike conditions. It is at this liminal juncture that the vowed Religious must stand—unashamed for what s/he espouses, and unrelenting in the prophetic stance s/he is required to adopt.

After the essential affirmation of God's absolute primacy in the unfolding process of creation, the liminal movement must then discern how to act. There are two basic Scriptural models: the Covenant of the Hebrew Scriptures and the Kingdom of God from the New Testament. Both involve models on how to relate rightly with God, in a co-creative adult relationship. And there is a second dimension frequently overlooked: how to relate rightly with God's creation. In this latter context, justice-making becomes the central issue.

It the ministry of Jesus, justice-making is largely about demolishing those religious and social institutions which favor some people over others, making some people frequently or permanently condemned to be outsiders. All the parable stories adopt this as a central theme, one that becomes incredibly subversive when we see one of the hated Samaritans being proffered as the model for Godlike inclusiveness, or a Jewish father abandoning all his indigenous religious and social privilege to welcome back a wayward son. And many of the parables challenge the hearers to a more creative use of the land as well as attending more conscientiously to the rights of those who work the fields and vineyards.

In our day, justice-making has become much more global and complex. While the covenantal model of the Hebrew Scriptures or the Jesus example of the Gospels can inspire and challenge us, the contemporary issues require contemporary strategies that can empower us to engage with the enormity and complexity of the contemporary world. The following are some of the critical and urgent areas awaiting our engagement and liminal commitment:

1. *Eco-justice.* As a human species our relationship with the creation we inhabit is dysfunctional and

unsustainable on several levels. We exhibit a disturbing level of ignorance about our home planet. Our exploitation and abuse of the earth is probably the single biggest cause of the meaningless suffering which millions of our species have to endure each day.

2. *Economic justice.* Money has become a god in its own right making compulsive consumerism (shopping) one of the deadliest addictions of our time. Money is the central ingredient in a cultural ideology that considers scarcity to be an enduring problem which humans try to sort out in terms of purchasing power. The leading economic theories of our time are based on gross distortions which inevitably lead to the destruction of creation's resources and thus fuel the irrational fears that already feed so much human consumerism.

3. *Political justice.* Most governments in today's world claim to uphold democratic values. This means a commitment to empowering people to be involved in the work of governance. Clearly, the vast majority of humankind does not, in any real sense, feel this sense of involvement. In fact the vast majority feels totally disempowered and disenfranchised. Even in Western so-called developed countries, many people feel at the mercy of government forces which they no longer trust, nor do they look to them for a better or more hope-filled future.

4. *Globalization.* The growing ineptitude of several national governments today is closely related to the fact that the traditional power and rights of national governments are being taken over by transnational

corporations. In the year 2000, of the 100 richest econo-mies on earth, 56 were major corporations which means that 44 were nation-states. The nation-state is rapidly becoming irrelevant, while national governments con-tinue to try and convince people that everything is pretty much as it was in former times. Globalization is pre-dominantly a Westernized movement, operating in many poorer parts of the planet with strategies remark-ably similar to the colonizers of former times.

5. *Violence (terrorism)*. In the millennial year 2000, over 11,000 people within the USA were killed in gun-related incidents. Our world today is in the grip of forms of violence, most of which are fuelled by irrational fear, which in turn seems to be maintained by an extensive sense of powerlessness. Educationally, politically and religiously, we face a very urgent task of trying to replace fear with trust, and powerlessness with empowerment. Otherwise, the spread of destructive violence could be-come the single most paralyzing influence of our time.

6. *Advertising*. We live in an information-saturated age. The extensive use of the Internet and of mobile phones, even in poor countries, bears witness to this. Everyday we are bombarded with massive amounts of information, much of which is of no practical use, and a lot of which is damaging to the human spirit. Our major educational systems, which are heavily influ-enced by capitalistic values, have not prepared or skilled us to deal maturely and responsibly with the propa-ganda and indoctrination which surrounds us on every front.

7. *Rights.* In the closing decades of the 20th century, the language of rights came to dominate the social and political landscape. (It has been noticeably absent in several religious contexts). The context is nearly always that of human rights, with, it would seem, a very poor awareness that human rights can only be respected and protected when planetary and cosmic rights are appropriately affirmed. And rights can only be promoted if duties are also embraced as a complementary value. Rights without due acknowledgement of corresponding duties can themselves become a subtle form of imperialism.

8. *Inequalities leading to poverty, oppression, marginalization, etc.* These are the issues—on a global scale—that come to mind when we think of justice. I place them at the end of the list because they cannot be addressed in any kind of comprehensive way until a number of the previously-listed issues are first confronted. The systemic forces undermining justice in our world today are fundamentally economic and political. The human dimensions cannot be addressed until we first confront the underlying cultural and systemic forces.

Proactive Liminality

I began my consideration of this vow by noting the link with the base chakra in the human energy field. Just as individual persons cannot realize the fuller potential of their God-given abilities without an appropriate grounding in God's creation, neither can the collective family of humankind without an appropriate grounding in the cosmic and planetary creation. Therefore, justice-making as a dimension of Christian mission (which is always to the whole—of humanity and creation) must embrace the more global horizons, complex and overwhelming though they may feel. Nor must vowed people be distracted from this urgent liminal responsibility by ecclesiastical disapproval of our political and economic engagements.

In the contemporary world, values are dictated primarily by socio-economic and political forces. We can only hope to change the destructive orientation by confronting not just the prevailing values but also the institutions that perpetuate them. Some attempts have been made to do this through various forms of protest, and through lobbying people who uphold and promote the dominant values. These strategies seek to change institutions from within. It often feels like pouring new wine into an old wineskin, and for this reason, it may lack the prophetic vitality that characterizes a more authentic liminal mode of redress.

For liminal witness, it is important to speak to the irrelevance of the old order, and name its impending demise, signaling the fact that institutions, like human beings, also die and fade into history. Getting institutions to face, what Brueggemann (1978, 46ff.) calls, the "numbness of death" is probably the single greatest liminal challenge of this, or any other, time. And then the liminal energy moves in the direction of being proactive rather than reactive. It begins to envision and name the alternative strategies and structures that are likely to be more conducive to augmenting that fullness of life for which Jesus lived and died. As Brueggemann (1986, 9ff) illustrates vividly, it is our grieving on what we need to let go of that liberates a more coherent energy empowering us to embrace something essentially new.

How does this new understanding of the vow relate to the former understanding? It brings forth in a much more conscious and explicit way the fact that all the vows are about values rather than about laws. That the redemptive power of vowed living is not primarily for individual salvation as rather for the wholesome (holy) functioning of all God's creation. The new understanding seeks to outgrow the narrow anthropocentric focus of previous times, situating the liminal people "in the world but not of it." And from a Christian perspective, the priority of the Reign of God becomes the primary motivating force. The goal is no longer perfection in some individualistic moralistic sense, but the active commitment to advancing the *pleroma* (completeness) that our God seeks for all creation, and not just for human persons.

SEVENTH BREAKTHROUGH:
VOWED COMMITMENT TO RIGHT RELATING

> *This is a moment when we need leaders to call one another and call our communities to heroism; to call us to risk, entering into those conflictual conversations that will connect us in trust and in hope to one another. . . to help us to face together the different, the other, the frightening and the unexpected.*
>
> DONNA J. MARKHAM

We used to call it the vow of obedience. It covered all aspects of leadership and governance in Religious Life. It began with the notion that Jesus was totally subject to the will of the Father and that this is the quality of discipleship we exercise by obeying those who have authority over us, namely our Superiors, Provincials and the ecclesiastical leadership of the Church itself.

The model is clearly defined in terms of wisdom from on high. God is the supreme unquestioned ruler, and rules hierarchically through the Pope, Bishops, and the various layers of leadership within Religious Life itself. Loyalty and fidelity are judged and valued by the zeal with which one honors and obeys those who govern, whether in person, or through the Constitutions and Statutes, the protection and implementation of which is the special responsibility of those in charge.

Within this model, obedience is the supreme virtue of the vowed life.

A Model in Crisis

I wish to suggest that this vow has been subjected to a great deal of distortion, and therefore, more than the other two vows, requires a deeper re-evaluation. There is also substantial evidence to suggest that, more than the other two vows, it is in the name of this vow that many Religious have been hurt, abused and victimized. It has left many feeling inferior, and emptied of their basic dignity and worth as human beings. The following are some of the key problematic areas that need fresh attention:

1. *A questionable image of God.* God is portrayed as a ruling patriarch. Many people do not believe any longer in this kind of God. Studies in the history of religion and in the Christian Bible increasingly suggest that this view of God is largely a patriarchal projection. For increasing numbers of Religious, women particularly, allegiance to this notion of God is becoming increasingly problematic.

2. *A sexist ideology.* Using the notion of the ruling God to evoke and validate one mode of governance is particularly disturbing to women of our time, and to an increasing proportion of men too. All the emphasis is on male qualities and masculine values, with Mary frequently portrayed as a humble, obedient, passive servant. Some scholars claim that this set of beliefs

has been the basis of the gross abuse of women and children over many centuries.

3. *A dualistic mode of governance.* Taken literally, which few Orders or Congregations do today, this is very much an arrangement of the governing ones vs. those who are governed, the active vs. the passive, the powerful vs. the disempowered. Dualisms aggravate the divisiveness of the patriarchal urge to divide and conquer. A dualistic culture is fundamentally violent, diminishing the potential for human growth and the graced capacity to work more creatively with God. Occasionally, those who end up being most abused and damaged are those who try to exercise this model of governance.

4. *Supports the culture of capitalistic competition.* Modern science highlights the fact that nature thrives on cooperation, not on competition (See the groundbreaking work of Lynn Margulis 1998). Prehistoric research also suggests that the cooperative, egalitarian mode is more conducive to authentic human growth than the values of capitalistic competition. Autocratic, dominant leaderships are certainly not congruent with nature; it is unlikely therefore that they would be congruent with God, the creator and sustainer of the natural world.

5. *Have we subverted an archetypal layer?* The word *obedience* is derived from the Latin, *ob-audiere*, which means to listen attentively. Might this not be an archetypal strand that has been subverted over time,

especially under the patronage of patriarchal governance? By reclaiming this more ancient meaning, we
begin to see what St. Benedict and several others considered obedience to be about: attending in a more discerning way to God's will for us, a process that Benedict
and Ignatius of Loyola considered to be primarily a
communal undertaking.

6. *Breakdown from within.* All over the contemporary world, we evidence the breakdown of authority
structures. All too easily we blame postmodernist influences. I suggest that a more discerning vein would
try to entertain the notion that the patriarchal system
itself is exhausted and even corrupt and is therefore
imploding from within. This is a liminal insight that
deserves serious and urgent attention.

The Liminal Challenge

To unearth the liminal significance of this vow, I
want to revisit Elaine Prevallet's rich insight aligning
the three vows with the three lower chakras (Prevallet
2000, 23ff). The third, sacral chakra symbolizes
power—that constellation of body-energies designed for
empowerment (of self and others), a center of creative
energy that is undermined when the channels for the
creative use of power are usurped or hindered. Using
this starting point has several advantages:

1. It locates the vow in the context of the *body.*
This is embodiment in that interconnected sense of the
Cosmic-Earth body from which human beings derive

their embodied identity, as a relational dimension that requires a body politic and a faith-based corporeality which Christians call the Body of Christ. All of which begs the question: what dynamics and structures are needed to empower the development of bodies in a creatively organic way? This may well be the supreme liminal question for this third vow.

2. The body uses the creative medium of birthing to channel and release its creative potential. An embodied vow must guarantee the ability to birth forth new life; otherwise it contradicts and stymies the very energy of creation itself.

3. It aligns the vow with energy-flow. Energy is the basic stuff of life, the raw material through which Spirit—divine and human—breathes and flourishes. How we channel this energy, and the systems we invent to mobilize it, becomes the concern for critical discernment, particularly for those entrusted with leadership on behalf of the human community.

4. The embodied context challenges the anthropomorphic interpretation we have imposed upon vowed living. Vowed commitment is not just about our relationship with God in the context of Church or religion. From a liminal perspective our vows ground us in the divine unfolding occurring throughout the entire breadth of God's creation.

5. Chakra-points are constellations of energy flow, not observable to the human eye, and therefore frequently dismissed as irrelevant in our excessively ra-

tionalistic culture. More accurately, the chakras are nodal points at which, and through which, energy flow assumes more productive ways of relating. Here we touch on another foundational quality of the vows: they are aids towards the right relating that God desires for all creation and that Jesus made a distinctive focus by adopting the rubric of the New Reign of God.

These observations give added credence to my suggested renaming of this vow as the *vow for mutual collaboration*. In the human body all the parts function in unison for the sake of the whole. And this includes the paradoxical dimension that a continuous death happens to facilitate the ongoing growth. Traditionally, we tend to think of the head governing the body with all the wisdom coming from the brain—a view that still carries weight in some sectors of the scientific community. Nowadays, we realize that the body flourishes through a highly complex interactive process located both within and outside the biological body. The governing wisdom is highly amorphous and multifaceted in nature and can only function meaningfully through a sophisticated cooperative endeavor.

Perhaps, this is a good definition for the vow of mutual collaboration: *a sophisticated cooperative endeavor!* It is not merely an organizational structure to keep order and control, less to dominate and rule over others. It is about mutual relating in which together we seek to mobilize the diverse gifts of the "body" for the good of everything in creation.

Liminal Structures

What, therefore, is the paradigmatic shift God is calling us to make as we seek to confront the crisis in governance and leadership that prevails in today's world? What are the implications for vowed Religious called to a ministry of liminal naming? And what are the structures we need to explore in order to facilitate the emergence of a new paradigm?

When we look at creation on the grand scale, we note the prevalence not of hierarchies but of holarchies. Let us begin by honoring that revelatory fact. If this is how the wise and holy Creator has designed nature and life, we are presented with a primordial reality that deserves our respectful and attentive discernment. Externally, it seems as if order prevails through descending layers from the most complex to the most simple. Biologists talk about "nested hierarchies" whereby units within a larger system behave like the larger system. Order from the top down seems to be the most widespread and effective structure adopted by nature.

Is this an observation of fact or a self-fulfilling prophesy in a world where we are all indoctrinated with hierarchical thinking? There is another model which nature uses extensively, but we give it little attention because our dominant way of thinking does not accommodate it. This is the holarchical viewpoint. It is construed around the philosophical principle of the *holon*, which states that every aspect of existence can only be understood within a context larger than itself. To understand me as an individual, one needs to know my family; to understand my family one needs some knowledge of my ancestry. That in turn requires an understanding of Ireland, my home country, which in turn belongs to a larger reality, Europe, itself an aspect of the Planet, which belongs to the Milky Way, and that requires the cosmos for a fuller understanding. There is no final frame of reference; the horizons of understanding keep expanding.

What are sometimes called the nested hierarchies are in effect wholes within wholes honoring the scientific principle that the whole is greater than the sum of the parts, yet each part is a whole unto itself. The good of each whole and the well-being of the greater whole requires a quality of interaction based on mutuality and cooperation. The relational potential of the holarchical model is immensely greater than the more linear approach of the hierarchical one. The holarchical model is a great deal more trinitarian than that of the hierarchical structure, as explored by a number of contemporary theologians.

Liminal witness seeks to honor the foundational holarchical nature of creation, itself a revelation of the foundational trinitarian understanding of God. In a word, creation is primed for relationality; organic life thrives through mutuality; humans flourish through cooperation, and not through competition. Liminal witness favors community over hierarchy, because it considers it more congruent with the divine plan for all creation.

In this context community serves a dual purpose:

1. To provide a context for group discernment, an attentive listening (*obaudiere*) to what God is asking of a particular group, and the individuals within it, in terms of the call to mission for the sake of the world.

2. To provide support and encouragement for the weighty and risky undertakings of those called to occupy the liminal spaces and serve as liminal catalysts on behalf of the people.

Structures of leadership, therefore, must reflect the primacy of the communal structure. These will tend to be forms of *shared* leadership, sharing out tasks and responsibilities in accordance with the call to mission of a particular group and the gifts of individual members. This is very different from an amorphous conglomerate adopting a utopian ideal where everybody is in charge of everything. Instead of transforming hierarchical power this chaotic system often creates a power-vacuum, leading to a new form of authoritarianism.

Collaborative Models and Patriarchal Structures

Religious Life struggles to incorporate a new leadership paradigm, a communal discerning one. It discerns the need to make this shift as a prophetic gesture to a world where patriarchal structures are proving cumbersome and irrelevant for the future. And those committed to this new vision are painfully aware of the obstacles we confront. Both the secular and ecclesiastical domains cling on unrelentingly to the old paradigm.

Patriarchal power tends to be a self-perpetuating ideology, which socially and politically wastes a great deal of time and money. It cannot and will not tolerate criticism of its existence and its mode of performance. Consequently, it will seek to undermine and eventually scapegoat those who challenge its hegemony. Those called to the liminal alternative will be persecuted to one degree or another. Misunderstandings from the secular sphere tend not to disturb us unduly, but the Church's allegiance to the patriarchal mode, and its hierarchical strategies is often a painful and baffling obstacle for Religious women and men of our time.

In our vowed commitment to mutual collaboration, there seems to be a growing sense of conflict between two irreconcilable models. In truth, we are dealing with an evolutionary transition that incorporates rather than destroys what has gone before. Whereas the older paradigm reserved power to those who governed from the top, and assumed that the rest needed to be governed, the disempowering effects of this model are now seen to be alien not just to true human freedom, but are even contrary to Christian faith itself. Power is primarily a gift given to empower, so that all can collaborate in the task of co-creation for the good of the whole body.

Today, most of the human species feel totally disempowered, forever struggling to overcome forces of alienation, poverty, oppression and slavery. Most frightening and disturbing of all, are the convoluted arguments through which marginalization has been justified in the name of political ideologies or religious subservience. All the religions portray a sense of the ruling deity, progressively seen for what it really is: a projection of the ruling earthly powers themselves. The God(dess) that humans have known and served for most of our time on this earth was an embodied earthly presence empowering from within, rather than ruling from on high. Even an incarnational faith like Christianity seems to have abandoned that more liberating image.

Many Religious in the Catholic Church today try to marry the two concepts into a more collaborative way of relating within the patriarchal hierarchical paradigm. In my opinion, this leads to a collusion rather than to an integration, and fundamentally betrays what is distinctive and prophetic in liminal witness. It is the task of liminal witness to name reality in a way that liberates deeper truth. The true relationality of God and of God's creation cannot be channeled meaningfully through hierarchical structures. And the prophetic calling of being lured by the mystery of God must speak to an appropriation of faith that transcends humanity's patriarchal need for domination and control.

The renaming, from a Christian perspective, needs to honor the primacy of the New Reign of God that calls all structures and systems to accountability in the name of egalitarian and inclusive values. Even several documents from the Catholic hierarchy claim that the primary purpose of the Church is to foster communion. Primary emphasis tends to be placed on communion with those in authority, with little attention to the communion among the rank-and-file membership, a prerequisite for true fellowship with those entrusted with leadership.

Dialogue is often proferred as the only authentic way forward, but sadly in the history of the Church there is little evidence for dialogue among adults, dialogue in the community of equals. The desire for control is mediated through a debilitating parental over-protectiveness. This is very different from the consultative process of seeking out people's feelings and opinions and incorporating those into final outcomes. True dialogue is about mobilizing the shared giftedness of all in order to discern the call of God in each new situation. And often it will mean moving according to the wisdom of the rank-and-file rather than that of those who govern.

Dialogue begins to break down when collaboration can only happen in terms of hierarchical expectations and control. The space for liminal movement has been restricted and the uniqueness of liminal discernment has been compromised. Collaboration essentially means forms and strategies of mutuality that honor an inner rather than an outer authority. The dominant wisdom is within the body, metaphorically located in the third chakra (in the stomach) rather than in the "head." The vow for collaboration today, involves a re-calling to what is more basic and foundational in how God relates with creation and how creation functions as an organic living structure. The priority of the divine and the priority of God's creation cannot be compromised.

The collaborative and hierarchical modes are fundamentally different, because hierarchy properly understood is a misplaced (or displaced) holarchy, and holarchies of their very nature are communal and collaborative. The vow for mutual collaboration operates out of a new paradigm, not for the sake of being trendy or postmodern, but because the collaborative approach is foundationally more creative for, and responsive to, the mutuality on which creation thrives at every level.

By embracing this vow, in this new interpretative vein, Religious seek to honor mutuality as a key value of creation and of God's involvement in creation's evolution.

EIGHTH BREAKTHROUGH:
CONTEMPLATING NEW HORIZONS
OF CONSCIOUSNESS

Many persons today sense that a large and critical change
in human consciousness is afoot.

ELAINE M. PREVALLET, SL

Philosophers of several ancient traditions inform us that action follows thought. As we think, so we act! Contemporary Eastern—Hindu and Buddhist-based—traditions emphasize the need for mindfulness, while in the West, we tend to adopt the more externalized, Greek-based wisdom of rational, logical discrimination. Whether the perspective is religious, philosophical or cultural, all seem to agree that the quality of our external behavior largely depends on inner dispositions related to attentiveness, perception and understanding.

Critics of contemporary culture agree and go on to suggest that humanity today suffers from an alarming level of external focus and fragmented identity. It is not that we have lost our capacity for interiority, but we are bombarded with sensationalized media forces that aggravate our spirits and set us in pursuit of sensual satisfactions with addictive intensity. We tend to be carried along by consumerism and hedonism, suffering from a diminished capacity to make discriminate choices and think in terms of long-term benefits.

Confused Consciousness

Postmodernist thinkers tend to laud this new dispensation. They see it as a breakthrough into a more free, fluid and organic way of relating to reality rather than the hegemonic structure of the old paradigm, with the emphasis on conformity to one supreme authority. It invokes the realism of the atomistic worldview governed by the Darwinian principle of natural section, and in some cases would attribute the desire for altruistic values to primitive religiosity. At the end, they suggest, we are left with a world where people are more real with each other, rather than more brutal in how we deal with reality.

Postmodernist views have a strong pragmatic appeal, especially for those committed to macro-economics and current capitalistic values. These generate the new wave of global colonialism, formally known as globalization. The philosophy of globalization thrives on a hedonistic type of pragmatism: live for today, make as much money as possible on what is currently available, and make as many people as possible happy in the process. And in this view, people's happiness largely depends on their ability to *shop*!

Shopping has become the postmodern religion par excellence! Our desires are dictated by the consumerist ideology of having more, consuming more, and enjoying it as much as possible. And identity has been subverted into a culture of fashion labels. No matter how poor one is, and irrespective of what other family members may need to meet basic needs, one must be seen to be wearing Adidas shoes and a Nike shirt. Rarely do we advert to the fact that these products are mass-produced by grossly immoral procedures including child labor and other practices exploitative of both person and planet.

Universally, a type of cultural myopia seems to have caught up with us. Our view of reality tends to be superficial and hedonistic. Capitalistic values reign supreme and to question their hegemony is considered immature, shortsighted, or simply out of touch with reality. People seem to think and reflect at a very base level, dealing with base needs in a rather unreflective way. Notions of more elevated reflective thinking are deemed fine for philosophers and religious people, but for the culture generally, these are considered to be quite irrelevant.

Some of the contributory factors to this confused culture need to be named with greater transparency:

1. Capitalistic cultures are quite adept at keeping people in the dark. They infiltrate media and educational systems to ensure that people think as they want them to think. While overtly, churches and religions condemn this strategy, subconsciously they collude heavily with this orientation.

2. All the mainstream educational systems thrive on reductionistic, functional ways of thinking and per-

ceiving. From a young age, we teach children to understand reality in a fragmentary and mechanistic way and we do a very effective job in making them fiercely competitive.

3. Although psychology enjoys a certain scientific status, it fairs poorly compared to the so-called hard sciences (physics, chemistry and biology). Consequently, the well-established notion of the subconscious—whether understood in Freudian of Jungian terms—carries little weight in the public forum of contemporary life.

4. As illustrations of number 3, political discourse, economic policy, legal procedure, and even theological doctrine, all take the rational, externalized mode of argument as the basis for their cultural and daily significance. Subconscious factors tend to be factored out. Internal motivation, feeling, emotion, intuition, tend to be dismissed as superficial, irrelevant non-essentials.

5. In a word, the prevailing consciousness thrives on base instinct, heavily seduced and indoctrinated by the prevailing consumerist culture. Several forces seek to dissuade people from thinking critically, and spiritual awareness has been substantially subverted.

6. A new type of slavery prevails today, a slavery of mind and spirit, in the face of which millions are growing restless, and the more restless they become the more dominant systems—and subtle consumerist forces—will try to allay their fears. But the restlessness will

prevail, birthing a new generation who, despite the opposition, choose to think for themselves and question the norms that are no longer credible. These are the catalysts that offer hope for a different future.

The New Paradigm of Consciousness

A new wave of consciousness is arising in our time. How we name and appropriate it is one of the supreme spiritual challenges now facing us, one that liminal people must not shy away from. Some of the indicators are relatively clear but will require at least another decade to honor them for what they really are:

1. The most obvious activating force is the proliferation of information, now doubling in months rather than years. Irrespective of poverty or ignorance, modern means of information, e.g., television, computers, cellphones, have infiltrated virtually every sector of humanity. Although the content and power of information is still heavily controlled from the top, its ability to get people thinking, reflecting, asking questions, becoming self-opinionated, expanding awareness, moves at an accelerated pace. Overwhelmed though we may feel by the masses of information we encounter each day, it is nonetheless changing us profoundly. This may well be one of those evolutionary shifts humanity undergoes about once every 10,000 years.

2. As more people become self-reliant in their ability to think and make decisions for themselves, they will throw off the shackles of guilt that have kept them

codependent in servile allegiance to older paradigms. Not alone are people beginning to think differently—and more critically—they are also becoming more proactive in shaping their personal and social realities in different directions.

3. At an accelerating pace, people are shifting allegiance from the mainstream institutions of Church and State—because the "information" out of which they operate is no longer perceived to be credible. It is simply not congruent with the emerging wisdom of the information explosion. Increasingly, people do not look to higher authorities for wisdom and guidance. They work things out for themselves, and network informally in order to build a different—and hopefully, better—future.

4. Several ancient cultures use the same word for mind and soul. The more we activate our capacity to think, even though it may be heavily influenced by the seductive propaganda of consumerism, the more we are awakened to deeper spiritual energies. A new spiritual awakening is beginning to arise, and for the greater part, seems to inform the living spirit much more effectively than formal religion.

5. Small but growing movements are emerging from the so-called hard sciences, inviting us to view reality in more spiritual and mindful ways. Examples that spring to mind include the Gaia theory, the creative vacuum, the theory of symbiogenesis, etc.

6. The study of consciousness commands the attention of several specialists in our time (see my re-

sume in O'Murchu 2002). Leading the way are those who consider consciousness to be a distinctively human characteristic, and for the few (like Daniel Dennett), restricted to the "machinery" (the *qualia*) within the human brain. However, an alternative view also prevails, the one I want to highlight in this final chapter as an issue of acute relevance for Religious Life in the future. This is the bold claim that consciousness belongs primarily to cosmic and planetary creation, human consciousness being one appropriation of what is essentially a cosmic, global quality.

7. Religious are called to be discerning people. Therefore, we need to ask: what quality of consciousness do we bring to processes of discernment? Is it an anthropocentric version over which we feel we have control, and through which we feel we can bring about a humanly controlled outcome, or is it congruent with that intrinsic wisdom which endows everything in creation including our human intelligence? These are weighty matters with substantial implications for the quality of our presence, thoughtfulness, and action in the world.

Building Up the New Consciousness

Clearly, many things in our world today are out of kilter. It is all too easy to apportion blame to leaders and organizations from which we expect leadership and guidance. Social scientists suggest that we get the leadership we deserve, and we tend to co-create those institutions which reflect the consciousness out of which our minds and spirits operate. Outer reality reflects our inner soulfulnesss, or lack of it, and as O'Donohoe succinctly states: "If we become addicted to the external, our interior will haunt us" (1997, 14).

Like many spiritual writers of the late 20th century, John O'Donohoe seems to consider our alienation to be an individual state of estrangement from God, arising from a dearth of spiritual meaning at this time. As a social scientist, I believe the problem belongs to a much bigger context. The problem is not with individuals but with the greater whole that constitutes the human landscape; our alienation is species-specific and systemic, rather than personal in the individual sense. And the alienation is not about distance from God, but about our estrangement from creation which was, and continues to be, God's first revelation to humanity.

Nor is it a spiritual problem in the more generic sense of the word. Our dilemma is very much the product of formal religion, which in many of its major expressions encourages humans to flee and abandon creation for the sake of life in a heavenly realm outside and beyond the earthly creation. This next-world projection, and the accompanying preoccupation with individual salvation, is endemic to the false consciousness that underpins so much human estrangement in our time.

If Religious women and men wish to offer the kind of creative future proffered by many of the great Founders and Foundresses; if we want to be the prophetic catalysts recalling our sisters and brothers to greater sanity and sanctity, we will need to attend conscientiously to our own levels of consciousness while being a great deal more vigilant about the quality of consciousness we promote in our engagement with life at large. I suggest that our sense of responsibility will be enhanced if we adopt the following strategies:

1. *A more integrated understanding of our human giftedness.*

We, humans are complex organisms with multiple levels of communal and individual endowment. We are not just physical, genetically-determined creatures with little depth of meaning beyond our overt biological capacities. Our capacity for socialization is real, so is our intellect and our need for spiritual meaning. We are creatures of feeling and emotion, with abundant examples indicating that we miss a great deal of what life is about when our analysis is governed solely by intellect. Developmentally, we are primed for relationship, for community and for creative interaction with cosmos and planet alike. It is grossly reductionistic to isolate the human from the non-human world.

2. *Our capacity for interiority.*

As far as we can trace into the dim and distant past, humans have always felt an attachment to inner mystery and an attraction to the power of the Holy. This became the basis of an incredible wealth of ritual and ceremony, often designed to honor the paradoxes of life and not just resolve them. The rational mind, so much a feature of recent millennia, seems to have dulled our intuition and our sensitivity to the mystery within and around us. Despite a great deal of rhetoric about contemplation and prayer, the contemplative gaze seems to have been subverted for much of what the anthropologists call the age of civilization (the past 5,000 years).

Spiritual writers of recent decades rightly identify a need and a growing desire to reclaim some inner space in our lives. We need to allow time just to be, in the solitude and stillness of mystery. We need time to resonate with all that cries out for attention from deep within. We need a gentle space so that we can begin to transcend the crazy jungle we have manufactured, bruising and battering our spirit on a daily basis.

The religions themselves bequeath us with a vast array of spiritual practices to regain this inner equilibrium. Both East and West have developed some well-tested meditation practices, accessed by millions in the past few decades. No longer is the wisdom of silence reserved to secluded monasteries. It is available today where it is most needed—in the noisy, restless furor of our suburbia and cities.

Religious specialists, often operating out of sectarian-based perspectives, warn against meditation practices and their "new age" dangers. These tend to be people who know little or nothing about the real worth of meditation. Assuredly, there are many religious charlatans around these days, similar to a vast array of dubious psychotherapists. But we are dealing with a culture where the adult is now invoked a great deal more extensively than in former times; adult people are capable of making informed choices and of rectifying matters if their choices are not working to their benefit. People who feel the need for a spiritual practice to cultivate interiority need to be encouraged in their search and not hampered by the ideological cautions of those who think they have a monopoly over spiritual truth.

3. A meaningful prayer-life.

A vast literature exists on this subject. How much is helpful to the contemporary seeker is a debatable question. The emphasis often hinges around strategies to turn the mind from affairs of daily life and to cultivate a relationship with God through verbal and ritual formulas as well as through silence and receptivity to God. Many people struggle with trying to get it right and spend an entire lifetime making heavy work of something which in its true nature is probably incredibly simple.

It baffles me how little attention we give to St. Paul's seminal insight that it is not we who pray, rather it is God's Spirit who prays in us (Rom 8:26-27). I find something deeply appealing, challenging and inspiring in this explanation of prayer. It defines prayer as a disposition of heart rather than as a set of exercises, verbal or otherwise. It puts the onus on God's creative Spirit and not on the human being, requiring of the practitioner not a masterful set of skills or prayer techniques but a radical sense of trust in the wise and Holy Spirit of God.

Instead, therefore, of set formulas, what we need to cultivate more than anything else is a capacity for spontaneity in our times of prayer, the ability to be able to articulate—whether in gratitude, petition, adoration, repentance—a sense of what God's Spirit is calling forth in one's life in the realm of daily experience, i.e., in the mystery of the ordinary. Assuredly, we need the support structures of words and formulas, of prayer times and structures, even of special places, but if these become the major focus of our praying, then I suspect the continuous provocation of the Spirit is in danger of being undermined.

Being prayerful people strikes me as being quite different from the exercise of saying prayers. What comes first is our prayerfulness—i.e., the Spirit breathing within—which may be a pleasing moment in a quiet church, but may equally be raging anger in the face of oppression and injustice, the passionate inner awakening that moves one to act for justice. After the awakening there may be a need for words, for rituals and possibly for regular structures. But instead of regular formulas there may be the greater and more urgent need for spontaneous outlets more congruent with the freedom and creativity of expression popularly associated with charismatic prayer groups.

What constitutes "success" in prayer, is named creatively by the late Henri Nouwen as a movement from delusion to reality. If my prayer is grounding me in a more real sense of life and its challenges, then it is probably of the Spirit. Sometimes prayer can bring sensations of mystical transportation, and some manuals suggest that this is prayer at its best. But might it not also be a grand delusion at its worst? The fact that it feels nice, does not in itself make it real. This is where the discerning skills of a spiritual guide become crucially important.

4. *Reflection and reading.*

Joan Chittister (1995, 137ff) draws particular attention to the development of the intellect among Religious in our time. In Religious Life, as in our culture generally, intellectual capacity is often confused with academic achievement. In a sense, our intellect is the handmaid of the soul. And we are all blessed with intellectual giftedness.

We nourish the intellect through the acquisition of wisdom, and not just through information or academic knowledge. Wisdom fares best when the endowments of intuition, imagination and reflection are well developed. The creative arts contribute richly to this development. So, too, does regular reading.

In the past, we strongly emphasized spiritual reading. Frequently this was equated with devotional perusal of the Scriptures. Theological materials were deemed to be for study and therefore not encouraged as material for spiritual reading. And critical commentaries on Scripture were certainly excluded from consideration. In a word, the desire was to keep the person spiritually subservient, loyal and faithful to the dominant religiously-validated culture. It was not a spiritual praxis aimed at mature adulthood.

I have deliberately listed meditation and prayer prior to my thoughts on reflective reading. A healthy and mature prayer-life awakens in us a hunger for intellectual growth. More accurately these are complementary rather than sequentially-structured resources for human and spiritual development. I want to place strong emphasis on reading, because it is the neglected element in many religious contexts of our time. Priests and Religious tend to be faithful to daily and/or weekly prayer schedules, but allegiance to regular, nourishing reading is quite sporadic, and serious theological nourishment is now much more widespread among lay people in the world than among Religious (men particularly).

5. *Contemplative discernment.*

The art of discernment is about availability to God in the heart of God's creation. In the discerning space, we strive to see as God sees, to relate as God relates and to act as God desires. Traditionally, the emphasis was on attentive submission to God; we were the passive recipients and God the active agent. Properly disposed, in humility and obedience, God could achieve things through us—often in spite of us—but rarely in collaboration with us.

This understanding carries many of the distortions of patriarchal ordering. It is a contemplative vision based on love of power rather than on the power of love. It is a projected, distorted gaze rather than an incarnational, contemplative one. It keeps God safe in the heavenly realm with humans struggling against heavy odds in this contemptible creation. Consequently, the privileged task of discerning engagement became the reserve of the holy few.

We now realize that discernment, like all God's gifts, is a grace given in freedom and generosity. And it is a task that none of us can do on our own. Nor is it merely about being aligned with God's will for us in terms of the holy things of life. Indeed, the most serious discernment for our time has to do with the ecological, political, economic and social forces that shape our culture. This is the arena where God's values are often under threat, where God's people are victimized in poverty and injustice, where God's will is jettisoned by those who play god for their own power and self-aggrandizement.

Throughout the closing decades of the twentieth century, the Catholic Church canonized several saints—more in a mere thirty years than throughout the whole of Christendom. The rationale was the simplistic conviction that this would help to increase holiness among the people and thus offset the adversarial forces at work in the world. This exhibits a rather primitive view of holiness, one that cuts little ice for adult reflective people of our time.

The call to discernment in this time involves a much serious study and analysis of a particular situation as it does prayer and spiritual reflection. All the elements are needed for authentic contemplation. Thomas Merton one time defined contemplation as the keen awareness of the interdependence of all things. It is about the big view that acknowledges the intricacies of life and culture and embraces a multi-disciplinary strategy in order to engage life more comprehensively. It certainly involves prayer and meditation, stillness and solitude, but as the life of Thomas Merton clearly reinforces, true solitude will always catapult us into the heart of God's creation. There, more than anywhere else, God's revelation continues to be made manifest and God's co-creative enterprise with humanity continues to take shape each day.

Several processes of discernment have been used over the Christian centuries. One approach I find useful and inspiring is the strategy of the Young Christian Workers: *See, Judge and Act.* All over the world, adherents of formal religions have a tendency to judge first; this is also an occupational hazard for Westerners in particular. The need to examine our perceptions and assumptions is not something we attend to as comprehensively as we should. Consequently, many of our judgments, and the actions that follow, address symptoms rather than deep causes. This is a plight that bedevils many political and ecclesiastical strategies of our time.

The capacity to see with depth and to honor the truth that belongs to depth is the contemplative dimension I describe above. The judging stage is about the incorporation of key values, and the exploration on how those values are best inculturated in diverse situations. When these two stages are appropriately honored, then the quality (and quantity) of the action is likely to be very different.

6. *Calling forth the reflective adult.*

What makes the philosophy of the Young Christian Workers—see, judge and act—so dynamic and rich is precisely its capacity to call forth the adult in people. This is a strategy best espoused by those who live by the adult values outlined in Section Three of this Chapter. Its implementation requires all the wisdom and insight gleaned from life's experience and the collective learnings of life's journey. This is a participative strategy which honors the mutuality of diverse gifts and not merely those who claim to have a monopoly over truth.

For Religious this requires an urgent review of formative programs and procedures. In many parts of the Catholic world, formation of initiates into the vowed life tends to follow patriarchal codependent models. Childlike subservience is highly prized with teacher and learner operating not in mutuality but in hierarchical order. Passive acceptance rather than adult engagement is the leading expectation, while adherence to standardized procedures takes preference over a healthy pluralism.

Religious Life is intended to be a form of adult discipleship, one particular expression of the discipleship of equals envisaged in the New Reign of God. The age of admission needs urgent review. If we wish to honor the adult that is being called forth, and promote in Religious Life forms of adult discipleship, then admitting people in late adolescence or indeed as young adults is not a responsible thing to do. People need to have had the time and space to experience life in the world and engage with adult challenges and responsibilities before considering the vowed life.

This also has implications for our vowed lifestyle and for issues of leadership and authority in particular. As indicated in previous sections, activating a sense of shared responsibility in communities of adults is not congruent with the hierarchical structures that have prevailed in the past. Communitarian and egalitarian modes of relating are more conducive to adult growth and development.

7. *Reclaiming our rightful place in creation.*

The new consciousness is very much about a reassessment of the role of the human in the process of creation at large. Even we do not concur with the notion that creation at large is imbued with consciousness—a view rejected by scholars in most disciplines—it is becoming much more obvious that human consciousness, as currently exercised, is not aligning humans with creation to the benefit of both or, indeed, to the benefit of either. The philosophy—and accompanying spirituality—of the past 8,000 years, conceptualizing humans as the masters of creation, is proving to be a tragic liability. Creation has been badly damaged because of our crude interference and there is a growing suspicion that we ourselves could be the primary victims of our own barbaric aggrandizement.

From the human perspective, three dominant scenarios prevail at the present time:

a) It is already too late. The damage is irreversible. Creation will continue to deteriorate to a stage where it will not be capable of sustaining human life. *Homo Sapiens* will perish, and with us the whole of creation. Even those who believe in this scenario, and they include some very serious thinkers, they hope against hope that there will not be a final calamity, that at the very least, our acceptance of this grim outcome will help us to die with some degree of dignity.

b) Things are in bad shape, but some miracle will happen and humanity will survive. This is a very unreflective, naïve view, offering a totally unrealistic sense of optimism. In a more benign vein, some believe that planet earth has been through crises before and survived them, so why not this one? The corollary often added here is that the Earth will survive, but humanity probably will not. We will become what some scholars call the "sixth extinction," paving the way for the emergence of a new species to succeed us.

c) For an estimated 90% of humanity, it is an issue they never think about. There is so much to be dealt with in daily life, these big questions are best left to "others" to deal with. Without wishing to be judgmental, I suspect this is the category of people against whom the words of Rev 3:16 might be spoken: "Because you are lukewarm and neither hot nor cold, I will spew you out of my mouth." These are the victims of patriarchy's disempowerment. I suggest it is these more than anybody else that need to be reintegrated into "the community of empowerment." (John Dominic Crossan).

The restlessness characterizing today's world is not that of disenchanted youth, nor disillusioned rebels. It is the pain and trauma of so many who feel they do not belong anymore: they do not belong in the government policies, in the economic ordering, in the violent streets of towns and cities; in dysfunctional relationships, in insipid churches and outdated religions. People feel out of place and yet, something deep inside suggests that a sense of place can be reclaimed (at least in theory). It is this intuitive sense that we belong to creation, and that creation wants to reclaim us as its own, that will engage the minds and spirits of many from here on.

Consciousness and the Liminal Threshold

Liminal witness is about renaming reality in a way that will make a difference, in a way that unveils deeper, liberating truth. This means mutual engagement with the cynicism and disillusionment which are widespread in our contemporary world. More importantly, it means striving to discern the awakening aspirations for meaning and hope, the aching cries arising from broken lives

in rich and poor countries alike. Perhaps most important of all, it means a massive reclaiming of human
and spiritual imagination so that we can begin to re-
create narratives that liberate and articulate what the
Spirit is striving to set free in our time. To this end, the
liminar is faced with some formidable challenges:

1. Can we be catalysts that facilitate the death of
the old while being midwife to the birth of the new?
This involves freedom to grieve, lament and let go! But
most challenging of all, it means transcending the denial, anger and bargaining of the grieving process, so
that we can be freed to "bury the dead." Only when we
have laid the old to rest—the old politics, economics,
religion, and patriarchal power games—will we be free
to embrace the new.

2. Meanwhile, we must start telling new stories,
alternative visions of how things might be for a different future. This future will be built on the shoulders of
the old, but true to authentic Resurrection hope, it will
contain dimensions that will be totally new and unexpected. In this task, liminal people face a daunting
challenge—not about evoking the future, but about
appropriating the past. For our mainstream institutions, the only past that carries credibility is that of
the past 5,000 years; the rest tends to be dismissed as
fanciful nostalgia for some long-lost golden age. This
cultural, historical shortsightedness has left us with a
stultified, truncated story ensuing in massive discon-
nection and alienation from the nurturing sustaining
creation to which we all belong.

3. This cultural retardation creates several hurdles as we seek to bring an enlarged vision to our petrified world. What the liminal people need to confront more than anything else—the material outlined in this section—is the shriveled-up consciousness with which the dominant culture perceives and understands. The rational, reductionistic, controlling mind has reaped havoc on imagination and creativity, leaving humanity with a grossly inflated will-power, constantly battling our way to "freedom" from our self-made crippling isolation. We need to start thinking afresh, thinking big, thinking globally and cosmically, thinking and seeing as God does. This is the heart of contemplation for our time.

If humanity wants to survive the 21st century, and reclaim a more wholesome place within the cosmic and planetary creation, the threshold witness of the liminal people is crucial. It will not be the first time—in the global history of Religious Life—in which those committed to the vowed life were drawn from the monastery to the world. And, I expect, it will not be the last time that we will surprise ourselves by the way we will have responded to the radical grace of divine giftedness.

ENDNOTES

Endnote 1: Throughout the text, the word *Religious*, with a capital *R*, refers to members of the vowed life, not to followers of religion which will be spelt throughout in *lower case.*

Endnote 2: In 1972, a French Jesuit, Raymond Hostie published *Vie et Mort des Ordres Religieux* (Paris: Desclee de Brower), proposing a new historical analysis of Religious Life in the Christian tradition. He argues that the vowed life tends to unfold in cycles of growth and decline, consistently within a timeframe of 300 years. The thesis was also adopted by two American Marianist Brothers, Raymond Fitz and Lawrence J. Cada (see "The Recovery of Religious Life," *Review for Religious*, 34, 690-718) who also explored the sociological aspects of this theory in Lawrence Cada & Alia (1979), *Shaping the Coming Age of Religious Life*, New York: Seabury Press.

As I indicate in O'Murchu (1991; 1998), I find this a profoundly inspiring approach to the history of Religious Life. Sadly, Church historians, who prefer objective, verifiable data, of a more factual nature, show little interest in this more imaginative analysis of patterns and cycles—further evidence to the poor understanding of our inherited history as Religious within the Christian tradition.

Endnote 3: The theory of Original Sin, and its link with Atonement Theology, is a complex question which feminists—and now many other theologians—feel a need to reconceptualize. I found the following books accessible and informative on the unfolding debate: Elizabeth Schussler Fiorenza (1994), *Jesus: Miriam's Child, Sophia's Prophet*, New York: Continuum; Darby Kathleen Ray (1998), *Deceiving the Devil: Atonement, Abuse and Ransom*, Cleveland, OH: The Pilgrim Press.

Endnote 4: Not a great deal is available on the story of female Religious in the other great religions. There are female monastics in Jainism, Hinduism and Buddhism, but they have been consistently overshadowed by the male traditions, and frequently have had to battle for survival. For further information on Jainism, see "Monks & Nuns" by Dr. Natubhai K. Shah (webpage: www.jaincentre.com); on Hinduism, Lynn Teskey Denton (2004), *Female Ascetics in Hinduism*, New York: State University of New York Press; on Buddhism, In Young Chung (1999), "A Buddhist View of Women," Journal of Buddhist Ethics, Vol.6, 29-105 (web page: www.jbe.gold.ac.uk); for a brief but informative overview of female Religious Life in Asia in general, see Abbott (1999, 189-202).

Endnote 5: In many Western countries, and in various missionary contexts of Africa and South America, Religious live singly or in pairs; this arrangement tends to arise as a response to ministry or apostolate. It is likely that this trend will continue and so it requires further reflection, consultation and deliberation on how such people can be integrated into communal structures. As Schneiders (2001) and others highlight, such integration is unlikely to happen unless and until we can offer greater flexibility in our notions and structures of community life.

BIBLIOGRAPHY

Abbot, Elizabeth (1999), *A History of Celibacy*, New York: HarperCollins.

Alexander, Bobby C. (1991), *Victor Turner Revisited: Ritual as Social Change*, Atlanta, GA: Scholars Press.

Brock, Rita Nakashima (1992), *Journeys by Heart*, New York: Crossroad.

Brueggemann, Walter (1978), *The Prophetic Imagination*, Philadelphia: Fortress Press. (1986), *The Hopeful Imagination*, Philadelphia: Fortress Press.

Chittister, Joan (1995), *The Fire in these Ashes*, Kansas City: Sheed & Ward.

Dupuis, Jacques (1997), *Toward a Christian Theology of Religious Pluralism*, Maryknoll, NY: Orbis Books.

Edwards, Paul. Ed. (1967), *The Encyclopedia of Philosophy*, Vol.6, New York: Macmillan

Fiand, Barbara (2001), *Refocusing the Vision: Religious Life into the Future*, New York: Crossroad.

Fiorenza, Elizabeth Schussler (1993), *Discipleship of Equals*, New York: Crossroad.

Foley, Nadine ED. (1999), *Journey in Faith and Fidelity: Women Shaping Religious Life for a Renewed Church*, New York: Continuum.

Fowler, James W. (1981), *Stages of Faith*, San Francisco: Harper & Row. (1984), *Becoming Adult, Becoming Christian*, San Francisco: Harper & Row.

Fox, Matthew (2000), *One River, Many Wells*, New York: Tarcher/Putnam.

Gardner, John (1981), *Self-Renewal: The Individual and the Innovative Society*, New York: W.W. Norton.

Gebara, Ivone (1999), *Longing for Running Water: Ecofeminism and Liberation*, Minn: Fortress Press.

Green, Joel & Baker, Mark (2000), *Recovering the Scandal of the Cross*, Downers Grove, IL: InterVarsity Press.

Haught, John F. (2000), *God After Darwin: A Theology of Evolution*, Boulder, Col. & Oxford: Westview Press.

Jonas, Hans (1996), *Mortality and Morality*, Evanston, Ill: Northwestern University Press.

Jungerman, John A. (2000), *World in Process*, New York: State University of New York Press.

Kennedy, Eugene (2001), *The Unhealed Wound: The Church and Human Sexuality*, New York: St. Martin's Press.

Kroeger, James H. & Peter C. Phan, (2002), *The Future of the Asian Churches: The Asian Synod and Ecclesia in Asia*, Quezon City, Philippines: Claretian Publications.

Leonard, Ellen M. (2002), "*Contemporary Theologies of the Vows*," Review for Religious, Vol. 61, 511-521.

Lerner, Gerda (1986), *The Creation of Patriarchy*, New York: Oxford University Press.

Lewis, C.S. (1960), *The Four Loves*, New York: Harcourt Brace.

Lorde, Audre (1984), "Uses of the Erotic: The Erotic as Power," in *Sister Outsider, Essays and Speeches*, Freedom, CA: Crossing Press.

Margulis, Lynn (1998), *The Symbiotic Planet: A New Look at Evolution*, New York: Basic Books.

Meyer, M.M. & L.G. Zucker (1989), *Permanently Failing Organizations*, New York: Sage Publications.

McNamara, Jo Ann Kay (1996), *Sisters in Arms: Catholic Nuns through Two Millennia*, Cambridge, Mass: Harvard University Press.

Moore, Thomas (1992), *Care of the Soul*, New York: HarperCollins. (1994), *SoulMates*, New York: HarperCollins. (2003), *The Soul's Religion*, New York: HarperCollins.

Nygren, David J. & Miriam D. Ukeritis (1993), *The Future of Religious Orders in the United States*, Westport, Conn: Praeger.

Nygren, Anders (1969), *Agape and Eros*, New York: Harper & Row.

O'Donohoe, John (1996), *Anam Chara: Spiritual Wisdom from the Celtic World*, New York: Bantam Books.

O'Murchu, Diarmuid (1991), *Religious Life: A Prophetic Vision,* Notre Dame, IN: Ave Maria Press. (1998), Reframing Religious Life, London: St. Paul's (2001), Vows for Non-Violence, Manila: Claretian Publications (2002), *Evolutionary Faith,* Maryknoll, NY: Orbis Books; Manila: Claretian Publications. (2004), Quantum Theology (revised edition), New York: Crossroad.

Phan, Peter (2002), *The Asian Synod: Text and Commentaries.* Maryknoll, NY: Orbis Books. (2003) *Christianity with an Asian Face,* Maryknoll, NY: Orbis Books.

Prevallet, Elaine (2000), *In the Service of Life,* St Louis MO: Loretto Earth Network (address: 590 East Lockwood Ave., St. Louis, MO 63119-3279, USA).

Quatra, Miguel Marcelo (2000), *At the Side of the Multitude: The Kingdom of God and the Mission of the Church in the FABC Document (1970-1995),* Quezon City, Philippines: Claretian Publications.

Rahner, Karl (1979), "*Towards a Fundamental Theological Interpretation of Vatican 2,*" Theological Studies, 40, 716-727.

Richo, David (2000), *Catholic Means Universal,* New York: Crossroad.

Ruether, Rosemary Radford (1992), *Gaia and God,* San Francisco: Harper.

SAFC (2000), *Starting Afresh from Christ: A Renewed Commitment to Consecrated Life in the Third Millennium,* Vatican City: CICLSAL.

Sahtouris, Elisabet (1998), *EarthDance: Living Systems in Evolution*, Alameda, CA: Metalog Books.

Sammon, Sean D. (2002), *Religious Life in America*, Staten Is.: Alba House.

Schneiders, Sandra M. (2000), *Finding the Treasure*, New York: Paulist Press. (2001), *Selling All*, New York: Paulist Press.

Schwartz-Salant, Nathan & Murray Stein, EDS. (1991), *Liminality and Transitional Phenomena*, Wilmette, Ill: Chiron Publications.

Sipe, Richard (1990), *A Secret World: Sexuality and the Search for Celibacy*, New York: Brunner/Mazel.

Swimme, Brian & Berry, Thomas (1992), *The Universe Story*, San Francisco: Harper.

Toolan, David (2001), *At Home in the Cosmos*, Maryknoll, NY: Orbis Books.

Van Kaam, Adrian (1968), *The Vowed Life*, Denville, NJ: Dimension Books.

VC. John Paul 2 (1996), *Vita Consecrata: Post-Synodal Apostolic Exhortation*, Vatican City: CICLSAL,

Wessels, Cletus (2000), *The Holy Web: Church and the New Universe Story*, Maryknoll, NY: Orbis Books. (2003), *Jesus in the New Universe Story*, Maryknoll, NY: Orbis Books.

Wittberg, Patricia (1991), *Creating a Future for Religious Life: A Sociological Perspective*, Mahwah, NJ: Paulist Press. (1996), *Pathways to Re-Creating Religious Communities*, Mahwah, NJ: Paulist Press.